W9-CNN-845

KINGS
OF LEON

SEX ON FIRE

KINGS OF LEON

SEX ON FIRE

MICHAEL and DREW HEATLEY

Reynolds & Hearn Ltd
London

First published in 2009 by
Reynolds & Hearn Ltd
61a Priory Road
Kew Gardens
Richmond
Surrey TW9 3DH

© Michael and Drew Heatley 2009

All rights reserved. No part of this publication may be reproduced,
in any form or by any means, without permission from the publisher.

A CIP catalogue record for this book
is available from the British Library.

ISBN 978-1-904674-05-4

Designed by James King

Printed and bound in Malta by Progress Press Ltd

ACKNOWLEDGEMENTS

Thanks to Nigel Cross for his crucial contribution
to the first two chapters, and Alan Kinsman for
compiling the discography.

This book is dedicated to all the bands who have
played 'Molly's Chambers' in bars across the world
- they know who they are.

PHOTO CREDITS

PAGE ONE: Mick Hutson/Redferns/Getty Images
PAGE TWO: Mick Hutson/Redferns/Getty Images
PAGE THREE: Ross Gilmore/Redferns/Getty Images
PAGE FOUR/FIVE: Tabatha Fireman/Redferns/Getty Images
PAGE SIX: Mick Hutson/Redferns/Getty Images
PAGE SEVEN: Mick Hutson/Redferns/Getty Images
PAGE EIGHT: Matt Cardy/Redferns/Getty Images

FRONT COVER: Gareth Davies/Getty Images International

CONTENTS

INTRODUCTION

**'The Kings of Leon's history is the epitome
of a mythological rock'n'roll story.'**
Rolling Stone

B y any standards, Kings of Leon are unique.
Consisting of three brothers and their first cousin,
all surnamed Followill, the quartet from a God-
fearing Tennessee background have conquered the music
world on their own terms in a manner reminiscent of the
Foo Fighters.

They have audaciously mixed elements of classic
rock, namely the Southern strains of Lynyrd Skynyrd
and the Allman Brothers, with grunge, garage and a very
contemporary attitude. The result is music that has found
a ready audience, ranging roughly between the ages of
15 and 50. Their music has also been used in several
significant movie soundtracks, the resulting exposure
accelerating their rise to superstardom still more.

The band have so far released four albums which have,

until now, proved more popular outside their native United States than within their home country. Once America fully wakes up to their promise, Kings of Leon (the name comes from the Followill brothers' father and grandfather, both named Leon) will truly have the world at their feet.

The band has been hailed by the British press as 'the kind of authentic, hairy rebels the Rolling Stones longed to be,' while their retro-chic look of long hair, moustaches and seventies-style clothing has also inspired comparisons to the Strokes, with whom they once toured and have now overtaken as headline attractions.

The Kings' record sales are matched only by their frequently lurid tabloid headline notoriety. Having broken through in Britain, they are huge in Australia and New Zealand, and are now finally beginning to conquer their own Middle American backyard.

Yet the Followills' rise to superstardom is all the more remarkable, given their backgrounds and early lives. The Kings' ride to the top is a tale so steeped in Southern Gothic Romance that you could hardly make it up – with, some would say, as epic a sweep as *Gone WithThe Wind*!

The saga starts out in the American South, home to so much great and influential music from Elvis Presley and Johnny Cash to Bo Diddley and Little Richard. Since its heyday in the seventies, when white-boy Southern rock was at its zenith and bands like the Allman Brothers, Lynyrd Skynyrd, Marshall Tucker, Grinderswitch and Wet Willie were among the most popular acts, that good ole boy blues boogie music has been out of favour – until now.

Kings of Leon (note the deliberate lack of a definite article) have turned a generation more interested in the Strokes and the White Stripes on to this fried-chicken flavoured, hard-stompin', redneck rock'n'roll. They may not be the first – recent acts as diverse as Kid Rock, Black Stone Cherry and My Morning Jacket have all flown the Confederate flag in their music – but they are certainly the one band to take it outside the USA and make it hugely popular in the UK and Europe, and now around the world.

The band themselves have always tried to distance themselves from being tarred with this label. 'We're not taking-our-shirts-off, barefoot, drinking moonshine, kicking our wives. We want to stay away from the Southern thing as much as possible.' But that's not something that's easily done. After all, to quote the old Dusty Springfield hit, three-quarters of the Kings of Leon literally are sons of a preacher man.

The four individuals' unorthodox background and beliefs, together with a lifestyle that kept them well away from popular music until 1997, when their father sensationally resigned from the church and divorced their mother, has led to some fascinating results. Subsequent exposure to sex, drugs and the rock'n'roll lifestyle has led to crises that have had to be resolved as a band and individuals – so the human story is as fascinating as the music itself.

Aretha Franklin, Otis Redding and Sam Cooke were also pastors' children, and while Cooke made a seamless transition from sacred to secular music, he also lost his life in the shotgun-fuelled aftermath of a liaison outside marriage. Money or salvation seemed to be mutually excusive in the eyes of many, and this ensured that the Kings of Leon has always been a band steeped in contradictions.

Yet in many ways that age-old dilemma has only added to their appeal. As one reviewer put it, 'Caleb has a model on his arm and money in the bank, but he's still haunted by his Bible-thumping' daddy. As long as the power of the preacher is out there, the boys will never get too comfortable. And God bless 'em for that.'

The closeness of the family bond is arguably a factor that keeps the Kings together – but it can also cause internal stresses and strains that have more than once threatened to pull the band apart. Backstage fights, brawls at awards ceremonies and even a fist-fight in the studio between elder brother Nathan and singer Caleb that led to real damage to the latter's arm have all caused headlines and threatened to derail the quartet's progress.

The band members make light of their disagreements, which have remained frequent despite recent success. 'I remember taking a class at high school called inter-personal communications,' Jared says. 'I learned about this wheel of abuse that involved couples arguing and then making up with champagne, flowers or candy.' Nathan continues with tongue in cheek: 'For us it's fight, flowers, chocolate, champagne, drunk, fight. On second thoughts, fuck the flowers and chocolate – it's fight, champagne, drunk, fight, champagne, drunk….'

There's also the very real possibility that Kings of Leon could burn themselves out through overwork. In 2009, Caleb said 'We've finally earned a year off but we're liking the buzz [of latest album *Only By The Night*] so much we're jumping back into it.' It's certain management, record company, promoters, venue owners, merchandisers and the thousands of people who depend on their activities to bring them their wage will be happy to hear that news, but if the goose that lays the golden egg is harmed then they could still conceivably become a 'what might have been' band. We have to hope that doesn't happen.

The most fascinating thing about Kings of Leon remains their back-story, and the feeling that there are forces at work we know not of that help them produce the magic music. Compare, for instance, the titles of their albums – *Youth And Young Manhood*, *Aha Shake Heartbreak*, *Because Of The Times*, *Only By The Night*. Detect a pattern?

Here's a clue – the answer lies not in the meaning of the words but their shape. Each title is five syllables long. 'We never want [a title] that isn't,' explained Caleb, adding that their 2008 release should have been *Only By Night* had they not altered the phrase from novelist Edgar Allan Poe (1809-49). Interestingly enough, the gothic wordsmith started life as plain three-syllable Edgar Poe…

Whether or not *Rolling Stone* was right to call it a mythological rock'n'roll story, Kings of Leon's history to date is short but fascinating. To start rubbing shoulders with royalty, just turn the page!

MICHAEL and DREW HEATLEY, SEPTEMBER 2009

CHAPTER ONE

BORN, NOT MADE

The two elder Followill boys, Anthony Caleb and Ivan Nathan, came into the world when they were born to father Ivan and mother Betty Ann in Mount Juliet. This small town is situated close to the home of country music, Nashville, in the western portion of Wilson County in the state of Tennessee. Younger brother Michael Jared was born in Oklahoma City. It's a family tradition that they go by their middle names.

The three brothers – Nathan (born 26 June 1979), Caleb (14 January 1982) and Jared (20 November 1986) – are the children of an ex-hippie, Neil Young-loving, holy roller. The boys all spent much of their formative years travelling through the Deep South from one church service to the next – revivals that could last anything between three days and 12 weeks.

The family was part of the United Pentecostal Church. Since its inception in 1945, this Church has become one of the fastest-growing sects within the Pentecostal movement. The Church is quite unusual in holding some non-traditional beliefs, which separate it from being called Christian.

The basic tenets of the United Pentecostal Church's faith include the belief that the ability to speak in tongues is a necessary indication of valid religious conversion. It shares with the 'Oneness Pentecostals' the practice of baptising in the name of Jesus Christ only. They believe that anyone who is not baptised in the name of Jesus only will not be accepted into heaven when they die. They reject the traditional concept of the Holy Trinity. They do not believe that the Godhead is composed of three persons: father, son and Holy Spirit. And they also believe that there is no salvation outside of the United Pentecostal Church.

The Followills' unusual and distinctive surname is supposedly of Dutch-German origin, but through the bloodline on their mother's side of the family they claim to be one-eighth Choctaw and Cherokee Indian. 'We're kinda mutts,' Nathan joked to *Mojo* magazine. Raised as God-fearing youngsters, the Followills criss-crossed the Southern states – Tennessee, Arkansas, Louisiana, Mississippi and Oklahoma – while their father preached the word of Jesus according to the United Pentecostal beliefs in churches and at revival meetings. 'We preached in some churches where literally we were the only white people in the room', Caleb would later tell *New Musical Express*.

When they were not in school, Betty Ann taught them their lessons. It was a little like living life in a bubble, as Caleb later pointed out: 'When we were growing up our parents didn't talk about politics and they never voted because they were all wrapped up in the religious life. The family listened to nothing but gospel music and didn't own a TV.' It wasn't all hellfire and old-fashioned religious devotion, though.

The family travelled through the South in Ivan's purple Oldsmobile, a vehicle as venerable and distinctive as the family itself. 'It would backfire', recalls Nathan, 'and we were so embarrassed that when we'd pull into a church, we'd have to kill the engine and coast into the parking lot.' He humorously adds that his dad could cause the car to backfire on command on occasions, such as when they might be driving past a building site. 'The guys would literally drop to the ground. I don't know how my Dad did it. He was a man of God, he was gifted.'

The constant frenetic travelling certainly had its drawbacks, as Caleb later reflected. 'People picture this great travelling lifestyle. There were moments that were awesome and then there were moments that we don't think were that awesome. I guess it was tough, and it shows more on us now than it did then, because at the time it was just our lives and we didn't know it was weird. If you made a buddy or found a girlfriend, it could never last long.' Talking to *New Musical Express,* he added, 'We were pretty young and travelled around all the time. We never stayed in one place longer than five years, so we never got to go to high school and make proper friends.'

The whole family would often have to sleep in the single backroom of the church itself. 'We'd have to use the preacher's shower', Caleb told *Rolling Stone.* 'It made you feel bad about everything you were doing.' As Nathan elaborated in the same article 'We'd come into town and there would be all these girlies around us. So every church we went to, we had to convince the guys not to whip our ass. The girls would be talkin' about us, and the guys would be like "Hell no! You're not coming into our church for one week and taking our women".'

The tight-knit religious fundamentalist atmosphere they grew up in did, however, have its upside. Each and every November, for instance, some 150 members of the Followill clan would get together down a dirt road in Albion, the poorest town in Oklahoma, for a family reunion on Thanksgiving Day. This ritual would later be celebrated in the song 'Talihina Sky', the bonus cut on their debut album.

Rumour has it that members of the extended family include criminals and drug-manufacturers in addition to preachers. As Nathan confided to *NME*, 'Dad's side of the family are real mountain people. They drink creek water and only eat stuff they've shot. A cousin built a house in the forest but the last time we went back it was nothing but a concrete slab. Their methamphetamine lab had blown up!'

Many of the Followills were also living in straitened circumstances, to say the very least. 'A few are housepainters', says Caleb, 'but a lot are unemployed – folks don't own a pair of shoes and you've never seen them wear a shirt. But all the time there's a pig cooking and no-one's any better than anyone else. They can all sing good…' Yet you wouldn't know there was any poverty as cousins, uncles and grandparents would line up on the banks of the creek drinking beer and whiskey, chewing tobacco and fishing for perch, catfish and bass.

The young lads would let off steam but, when it was time to go, they were happy to be on the move again. 'We have a blast because we leave after a week – but the people there, they don't leave. We've been year after year and you see the same process. Different high-school kids pregnant. Here comes the new kid and the same thing happens. Drugs or whatever. Everybody goes through the same shit and no one ever sees it coming.'

It's a wonder, given their mother's sisters all married preachers, that the boys didn't end up following in the family tradition too. Legend has it that as a nine-year old Caleb wrote his first sermon – 'Why beg for bread when you're living in a wheat field?' – though he never delivered it!

'As a little boy', Caleb told the *Guardian*, 'I thought all of us would (be preachers). Every little boy wants to be their dad, and then later on they want to be the opposite of their dad. All our friends would go to bible college after high school. Two years learning how to preach. That was just what everybody did. And we pretty much knew that was what we were going to do, too.'

And contrary to their womanising, coke-snortin', Jack Daniels-drinkin' decadent rock image, the Kings grew up as sweet-mannered kids who, like all good country boys, went hunting, shooting and fishing. When it came to killing anything, they felt more than a twinge of guilt – like the time Caleb shot a woodpecker and Jared accidentally shot a rabbit. He tried to revive it with a slice of cold pizza, hoping it might recover, 'but it just flipped over and died. I swear to God, I felt bad about it.' As Caleb told the *Telegraph*, 'We didn't really look at (our upbringing) as restrictive at the time. We were pretty good kids, really. We would only get in trouble by doing stupid shit….'"

The boys would later be at great pains to put the Southern background into perspective. Jared stresses 'I don't think we're *that* Southern. We're not racist, we don't tote guns around and do stupid bullshit like that – we're just normal people.' Older brother Caleb adds, 'Morally we were raised the right way. We're good guys, we open the door for a lady and all that, so in that sense, yeah, we're Southerners.'

It was the church that gave them their basic musical grounding – they learnt to play piano, organ, guitar, bass, drums and even horns at gatherings at their father's church in redneck Mumford, Tennessee. Nathan played drums at services from the age of eight alongside his father on bass and mother on piano, while worshippers danced in the aisles to their 15-minute recitals. As he later observed, 'Most people think the music is reserved, but there's organs, pianos, basses, drums, horns. It's like black gospel music. It's a full-on Al Green, Aretha Franklin-style service.'

Though he found the gospel music uplifting and intoxicating and liked to sing as part of the church congregation, Caleb was far from keen to sing publicly, even when entreated to do so by his mother. 'When I was really young', he told *Mojo* magazine, 'I was always the life and soul of the party, the clown. But around 10 years old, I don't know, I just became really shy.'

Fortunately, three years later he finally got over this hang-up and managed to perform a gospel standard 'Love Lifted Me' in a church in the heartlands of Oklahoma. This was a real Paul on the road to Damascus moment. 'It was almost like I broke down that shyness for those three minutes, and then went back to being myself again', he confessed to *Mojo*, 'but it felt really good to me.'

Their strict fundamentalist upbringing meant that, as kids, the Followills were not allowed to listen to any secular music, only gospel – though when they did, as Nathan would later observe, 'we wouldn't have gotten caned or anything, but there would be a lecture.' And it didn't necessarily mean that they saw only the sweetness and light associated with a Christian life.

'People think that, because you grow up as preacher's boys, you see only the good side of life', Caleb would later opine to *Mojo*, 'but really we saw a lot of the bad because whenever we went to different churches, the pastor would always let my dad know what was going on. Like so and so used to be a prostitute…'

While Betty Ann was unwavering in her dedication to the spiritual life, and thought of rock'n'roll as the devil's music, their father, it is alleged, would let the boys listen to all kinds of rock records in the car by artists such as the Rolling Stones, Neil Young and Bad Company, when she wasn't around! Indeed this unorthodox itinerant lifestyle was the perfect training for their later life as international country-hopping rock'n'rollers.

'The way we grew up, it was me and Caleb and Jared in the back seat of a car, all three together all the time', Nathan told *Mojo*. 'Now we're either on a bus together, on a plane, at a hotel bar or playing a show together. We wouldn't be the band we are today if we'd grown up "normal". Many bands break up because they're not used to being so close to someone so much of the time.'

After he was given a radio for Christmas one year, Caleb would listen to pop music on the sly. 'I used to sleep with the radio under my pillow and listen to oldies', he told *Rolling Stone*, 'Other nights I'd get a cassette of my Dad preaching and listen to that. I'd wake up with the worst cricks in my neck from sleeping on that radio.' At first he'd tune the dial to oldies stations and Ben E. King's classic soul number, 'Stand By Me' became an early favourite but it was listening to the old Tommy James and the Shondells hit 'Crimson And Clover' in his uncle's car that really turned his teenage head – a watershed moment. It is this song that he attributes to making him pay attention to pop music generally.

'It was the most amazing song I'd ever heard',

he admitted to *Mojo*. Not even his uncle explaining the explicit content of the song's lyrics could put the youngster off. 'He said, "It's about someone taking a girl's virginity in the grass – that's the crimson and the clover." I was like, wow, even this music is hell-bound. But as soon as I heard that song, I knew I wanted to do something with music.' The rot quickly set into his teenage mind, as he later admitted on US TV. 'The next day I got into the car with a buddy at school and he put on some Pearl Jam… I went, "Wow, there's obviously a lot out there I need to experience".'

After Jared was born, the family settled down in rural Tennessee. (Nathan calls it *Deliverance* country, as per the 1970 John Boorman film of the same name which depicted four city slickers challenged by the brutal landscape and its equally brutal inhabitants.) For the first time the Followills were able to put down some roots. The religious reins also slackened around the boys, and acts of rebellion inevitably followed. In one of these, Caleb and Jared shot out the windows of their father's 4x4 with BB (ball bearing) guns.

And more was to follow. When he was 14 Caleb smoked marijuana for the first time in Henderson, Tennessee with his cousin Peanut. 'I was with Peanut and we were in a graveyard,' he says. 'I was like "I don't feel it", but when we got home I was eating a bunch of chicken tenders. Peanut said, "What the fuck, man, you're gonna kill your buzz." That's when I realised, "Maybe I *am* feeling this!"' The boys would also hold wild parties at their parents' place. When Ivan felt enough was enough, he would put jalapeno peppers in the microwave. The fumes burned peoples' eyes until they vacated the premises!

Even young Jared had his wild moments – he was notorious around the local neighborhood for riding his scooter, naked! 'I'd wear a T-shirt', he jokes, 'so I wasn't

completely naked. I'd be casual but naked from the waist
down.' Unlike his older brothers, Jared actually attended
state schools and enjoyed a more conventional childhood
– 'That's why I'm so much cooler,' he'd later parry.
And mixing with other kids meant that his own musical
horizons broadened and he was opened up to alternative
rockers such as Weezer, Joy Division and Pixies. These
mixed in with the likes of bands such as Television,
Credence Clearwater Revival and the Velvet Underground
to produce the musical motherlode the Kings would draw
upon. As Matthew explains, the sudden exposure was
nothing short of life-changing: 'We couldn't watch TV
and we couldn't listen to rock'n'roll. I didn't know who
Bono was till I was 18.'

The blinkers were off, and the young men were all
but blinded by the possibilities – even though their own
music-making abilities were as yet untested. 'When
you grow up listening to rock music all the time, I don't
think you can really grasp how amazing some of these
songs are,' said Jared. ''But when you hear them for the
first time when you're 16, or 18, or 19, it's going to do
something to you, and that's what happened to us.'

Sadly, in 1997, the boys' world was shattered. Betty
Ann and Ivan – who would subsequently go under the
moniker of Leon, his middle name – split up. In the eyes
of the Pentecostal Church this was an even bigger sin that
it was in Christian circles at large. Leon was drinking
heavily 'because his nerves kind of got to him' says Caleb
– and, accused of philandering, Ivan was forced to quit
the church. 'I wasn't defrocked, I resigned,' he later said.
He gave up preaching and went off to paint houses in
Oklahoma, where 'you're guaranteed a day off every
time it rains.'

While he didn't miss the daily grind of religion, like most teenagers Caleb took the break-up of his family hard. 'Same as it is for anyone whose parents split...it was one of those moments when I started questioning what was real and what wasn't.'

Big brother Nathan took it just as hard. 'Our parents' divorce shattered the whole image of this perfect little existence the outside world couldn't touch and couldn't pollute. We realised that our Dad, the greatest man we ever knew, in our eyes, was only human. And so are we. People are gonna fuck up,' he confided to *Rolling Stone.* 'They're gonna want to experiment with drugs, have premarital sex. This whole new world was open to us.'

Indeed Nate remembers it as 'basically like a new beginning. I was about 18 and Caleb was 15, the natural time for us to turn into rebellious little dipshits.' They began going out to clubs together, Caleb using their 24-year-old cousin's ID. ''We would tell all the girls we were on the golf team at some university, or that we were doctors', Caleb joked.

Nathan graduated from the Christian Life Academy, a now-defunct private school in Henderson, Tennessee. Caleb meantime dropped out of school mid-senior year. Nathan went on to study sports medicine and physiotherapy at college in Henderson ('so he could work with female softball players'), while Caleb started working on building sites over in Jackson.

Their lives, however, were about to take a dramatic turn...

CHAPTER TWO

BAND AID IN NASHVILLE

A s the first year of the twenty-first century came
into view, the two eldest Followill brothers found
themselves living in the Nashville suburb of
Mount Juliet with their mum and young sibling Jared.
As Nathan would later tell *Mojo*, 'Me and Caleb just got
bored with our normal lives.'

In common with most youngsters of that age, a lack of
ready cash was severely curbing their leisure activities.
But Nathan was delighted to find that help was at hand.
'In Nashville, we met a guy who said he just got paid
$2,000 for writing a cheesy-ass country song. We were
like: "Really?" We needed money to buy dope and we didn't
want to work at the mall, so we started writing songs.'

The brothers embarked on duo gigs around the bars
and clubs of the city, and started to write their own songs.
Nashville is of course the capital of country and their early
efforts drew heavily on this kind of music. 'I've always

related to country music,' Caleb would tell *Mojo*. 'I listen to Merle Haggard all the time. Country music, it just takes you back. It doesn't matter if I'm in Germany on a bus – if I'll listen to a country song, I'm immediately 12 years old and with my family.'

Nathan looks back at their early efforts as 'horrible nineties Everly Brothers stuff', but Caleb has fonder memories of the period. 'Once I heard the Stones and Dylan,' he told *Rolling Stone*, 'I thought "My God, why should we be held to our own experience? Why not do like our Dad did as a preacher?" Every day he saw something that inspired him and told a story about someone different. I had to put myself in other people's shoes.'

One summer's night in 2000, Nathan and Caleb decided to drive into Nashville and sample some of the devil's finest music. They were travelling straight from Church and still sporting their best Sunday attire when they headed for the legendary musical hotspot known as the Bluebird Café. Located at 4101 Hillsboro Pike in Nashville, the Bluebird is a restaurant cum concert room founded by Amy Kurland, back in the eighties. The venue prides itself on providing a quiet atmosphere for writers and artists to perform their songs. Among the countless writers and singers who have graced the stage of the Bluebird are Steve Earle, John Hiatt, Bob Mould, Vince Gill, Guy Clark, Kris Kristofferson, the Indigo Girls, John Prine, Townes Van Zandt and Arlo Guthrie. Over the years it has cemented its reputation as one of the venues singer/songwriters aspire to play in Nashville.

That evening, Nathan and Caleb encountered singer and guitarist Trey Boyer. Though he'd never met them before, he was intrigued enough to ask the pair round to his place the following night to play some of their songs for him.

'When we started to play', recalls Caleb, 'we could see his face light up.'

Boyer, a gifted singer/songwriter who specialises in rootsy Americana, folk and country, takes up the story: 'I was born and raised in Atlanta, Georgia. I started playing music in high school, but didn't start playing out publicly until college. I attended the University of Georgia which is located in Athens. This is where I really cut my teeth in music and "found my sound". I released a couple of EPs while in college.'

His first band after college was called Dimestore, and they released a full-length CD in 1997 called 'Vanishing America.' Not long after the release, however, the individual members all went on to separate projects. It was at that point that Trey Boyer decided to move to Music City. He continued to play and tour and while in Nashville, released a CD called *On My Way*.

Not for the first (and certainly not the last) time, Trey recalls his first meeting with the Followills. 'I met Nathan and Caleb at the Bluebird Café in Nashville back in 2000. I was playing the Sunday Night Writer's Night and they approached me after my set. They said they liked what I had played and wanted to know how to go about getting a gig at the Bluebird. They had just moved to town, I think they had been in town less than a week, and this was their first excursion to check out the Nashville music scene. When I told them they had to audition to play the Bluebird Café they informed me they wrote songs, but only Nathan played an instrument (drums). We traded numbers and I told them I would put some music to their stuff and help in any way I could.'

The first night they came to his house Boyer's girlfriend (now wife) Susanne was there. Susanne is also a singer, so the quartet hung out in the carport and played each other tunes. 'When we first heard them sing it was readily apparent to Susanne and I that they had something special' Boyer recalls. The Followills were singing songs they had written acappella and the songs were complete with verse, chorus and bridge.

To Boyer's ears, the Followill brothers obviously had raw talent. 'The songs had tight harmonies and both their voices were very soulful. I remember being impressed with their ability to write without accompaniment. I was able to put a guitar part to what they had written and soon we auditioned for the Bluebird and got a slot. Their early songs had a definite country influence, but it was constantly evolving. I would play and Nathan and Caleb would sing. I am sure there was the genesis of a song in there somewhere.'

The Followills and Boyer played several local venues in Nashville together. One of the first was the Bluebird. 'I think that was their first real taste of singing in front of an audience,' he recalls. 'You could tell they were nervous, but once they started to sing everything just clicked. Whether we were playing in front of an audience in a bar or some PR guy at a record label it was always cool to see the reactions to Nathan and Caleb. Everyone always lit up when they heard them sing for the first time.'

Trey Boyer was the first of a number of significant individuals who helped give the Followills an early step up the ladder to fame and fortune. 'When Caleb got his first acoustic guitar, I showed him some basics and wrote out a bunch of chords to help him get started – E, A, G, D, B7, etc.' And even when they weren't doing music together Boyer still liked to socialise with the brothers. 'I did spend some time hanging out with Nathan, Caleb and Jared at their mom's house. Mrs Followill was always very sweet and welcoming to me,' the guitarist recalls.

The duo worked for a brief period of time with a small label/management group Pistol Creek Productions, spending their time with them mainly singing at rodeos. They also were members of the West Tennessee Mass Choir for a short period, with whom they sang falsetto harmonies. Life even then wasn't without incident. One time the pair flew to San Diego for a songwriters' convention. They were staying with a friend of a friend and, before setting off for the convention hall, smoked a joint on the outdoor wooden deck area. Stoned, the brothers didn't put the 'doobie' out properly and left it smouldering – later in the day they heard that the whole deck had gone up in flames!

Trey Boyer then introduced the brothers to an entertainment lawyer friend, Kent Marcus, who worked for Zulmwalt Almon and Hayes. 'I felt that, with his connections, we could open up some doors on Music Row. Every time we went out to play at a record label or publisher things went great. People always responded well to the music and the brothers.' Soon they began a tour of Music Row, playing for major labels from Sony to Dreamworks and anyone else that would listen.

As fate would have it, it was through Zumwalt, Almon and Hayes that the brothers were introduced to the formidable and veteran manager, entertainment lawyer, producer, publisher and booking agent Ken Levitan. This was a man who had developed an international reputation as one of the most successful entrepreneurs in the US music industry. As president and founder of Vector Management, his artist roster boasted such legendary and diverse acts as Emmylou Harris, Lyle Lovett, Hank

Williams Jr, the B-52s, Ben Folds Five, John Hiatt,
Michael McDonald, Lynyrd Skynyrd, Trisha Yearwood,
Trace Adkins, Jonny Lang and Patty Griffin. Levitan's
musical achievements had been recognised nationally in
1998 when he was awarded a Grammy for producing
The Apostle soundtrack.

The son of a surgeon, Levitan hailed originally from
Brooklyn, New York. His father had dabbled in the
entertainment industry in his spare time, managing
members of the Four Seasons and Canadian country
performer Ronnie Prophet before moving into film
production. His father's enthusiasm must have rubbed
off on him because, while attending Vanderbilt University,
Ken ran the school's concert committee, booking acts such
as Carole King, Genesis, Stephen Stills and Hall & Oates.
Having completed his studies there, he went on to work as
a booking agent for Buddy Lee Attractions, working there
with the likes of Willie Nelson, George Strait and Jerry
Lee Lewis.

In 1983, following his graduation from the University of
Dayton's School of Law, Levitan returned to Nashville and
helped secure record and publishing deals for Lyle Lovett,
John Hiatt and numerous other singers and songwriters. In
1990 he established a management company to represent
Steve Wariner, Nanci Griffith and New Grass Revival. He
quickly became a full-time manager and joined forces with
Will Botwin to manage Griffith, Lovett, film composer
Mark Isham and others. Their publishing company,
Crossfire, worked with Crash Test Dummies, Deana Carter
and Matthew Ryan.

In 1996, Levitan was tempted away from management
by the opportunity to run Rising Tide Records, a subsidiary
of Universal. He signed Dolly Parton, Matraca Berg, the

Nitty Gritty Dirt Band, Delbert McClinton, the Buffalo Club and Rebecca Lynn Howard, in the process enhancing his growing reputation of musical integrity and furthering his music-industry knowledge. 'I wanted to learn the other side of the business,' he said. 'It was a good challenge to start a fresh record company.'

A casualty of the Universal-PolyGram merger, Rising Tide was closed in 1998. After helping his wife, Gloria Dumas, win her campaign to be Davidson County General Sessions Judge, Levitan returned to the music business in the autumn of that year and re-activated Vector Management. Speaking about his goals at Vector, Levitan commented: 'You have to balance the creativity and the business side to really make sure the artist maximises his or her own goals. We really want to try to build box sets and long careers instead of one-hit wonders. We are in a time when everything is really quick-hit oriented. We try to take a long-term marketing approach.' On paper, at least, this offered the perfect environment to nurture two young musicians with stars in their eyes!

Levitan in turn introduced Nathan and Caleb to an old colleague, musician and producer Angelo Petraglia. Born on 5 May 1954 in the Bronx, Petraglia was raised in Pelham, New York. His father was a janitor, his mother a bookkeeper. By third grade Angelo was playing guitar, but it was his meeting with drummer Billy Beard while studying visual art at New England College in Boston that eventually led to a successful band, the Immortals.

Through his publishing deal with the Immortals, Angelo made some Nashville connections and, at length, went down for a month-long visit. 'I couldn't believe it,' he says. 'I wrote 15 songs with people in four weeks. Boston is a great music town, but the music community here was

31

really refreshing to me.' Totally enraptured by this city in Tennessee, he sold everything he had in Boston and moved to Nashville in April 1993 with just two guitars and a backpack to his name.

After four months schlepping round record-company offices, Angelo signed on with PolyGram, which subsequently merged with MCA Music to become the Universal Music Publishing Group. He was then introduced to George Ducas, who recorded three of Angelo's songs and employed his services as guitarist on his first album. What followed was a classic run of golden connections. The album's producer, roots country eminence Richard Bennett, was also making Kim Richey's first record.

The pairing of Angelo and Richey quickly turned out to be a match made in musical heaven, as Petraglia co-wrote three songs on her debut record for Mercury. They also co-wrote the Grammy nominated song 'Believe Me Baby (I Lied)', for Trisha Yearwood. When it was time for Richey to make her second album, Angelo had played a part in writing so many of the songs that he became a natural choice for producer. The result was the critically acclaimed *Bitter Sweet*, a beautifully composed and textured work.

Angelo toured with Richey to promote the record, success led to further success and he soon found himself producing and writing *One Big Love* for Patty Griffin, later recorded by Emmylou Harris and included on her Grammy award-winning record *Red Dirt Girl* in 2000. He'd go on to write for such respected artists as Martina McBride, Tim McGraw, Sara Evans, Lee Ann Womack, Brooks and Dunn and Jessica Andrews.

With his extensive, seasoned experience both in country music and indie rock, Petraglia was a genuine find for musical greenhorns Nathan and Caleb Followill. Not only did he have a music room stocked with vintage guitars but he also owned a formidable collection of vinyl LPs. The Followills' limited knowledge of rock's rich history was about to be expanded a thousandfold. Petraglia and the boys hit it off immediately and they were soon embarking on what Caleb called 'a crash-course in the history of music.'

Opening their heads to the likes of the Velvet Underground, the Clash, Dylan, Rolling Stones, New York Dolls and Sly & the Family Stone, Angelo poured in all the good stuff. Describing it similar to 'the Smithsonian Institute of gypsy hash rock', Nathan told *Mojo*, 'he'd break out a nice Scotch and we'd sit there and smoke while he'd just blow our minds.' For his part, Angelo takes credit for 'turning those guys on to the Rolling Stones and a lot of the older, raw rock'n'roll stuff.'

Petraglia's initial introduction to singer/guitarist Caleb and drummer Nathan had come through his publishing company as potential songwriting partners. 'There was a misconception from the beginning,' he'd tell Gibson Guitars *Lifestyle* magazine, 'where some people thought this band was put together, which is so untrue. I mean these guys have so much talent (and), whether it was in the beginning very raw, talent is talent. To me, it was just guys that I hit it off with and dug making music with, and the writing was really cool. At first when I met Nathan and Caleb it was just pretty obvious that they had a thing. They had a sibling thing that was pretty powerful, and when they sang they had the sibling harmony that's hard to get anywhere else. That was pretty special, there, right off. They just had a lot of soul.'

Angelo believes that their unusual family background contributed to the raw potential that he recognised soon after meeting the pair. 'They kind of grew up in this whole Pentecostal background,' he explained, 'and that was their experience in the world. People have heard (this story) a million times, cruising around with their father as he was preachin' and stuff travelling the South, going to all these church meetings. But, initially, to me, it was like they had a pretty old soul when it came to music.'

Having worked with so many different artists and in different genres of music, Petraglia was a key ingredient in shaping the early Kings of Leon sound, the catalyst they had been searching for. Not only did he introduce them to an expansive catalogue of music but also quite literally placed a bevy of classic rock guitars in their hands. They had access to his vast collection of vintage Gibsons and Epiphones.

Hanging out and jamming with the man from the Bronx, Nathan and Caleb naturally began working up songs. 'The music we're drawn to is usually based upon stories', Caleb would tell *Mojo*, 'it's how we learnt to write songs. People from the past were some damn good storytellers – those old blues about love, loss, murder and religion. We do that but we take it to a different level. We're a younger generation, so the way we look at it is totally different.'

By now, although he was yet to be formally involved in their band endeavours, youngest brother Jared was beginning to have some influence on his older siblings' music. 'I started getting into the Pixies, Talking Heads and Velvet Underground, then I heard the Strokes and Black Rebel Motorcycle Club and White Stripes, cool stuff that was modern' he says, 'and once the Strokes came out, I put a little birdie in their ears about forming our own band.' While Petraglia played them classics from rock's illustrious past, their little brother was turning them on to contemporary underground acts like Neutral Milk Hotel, the Clinic and Built to Spill. All these diverse influences would coalesce into the music that found its way on to the band's debut EP.

Nathan takes up the story, telling *Mojo* magazine: 'We were evolving as songwriters and we'd got 20 songs that no-one else was gonna cut, because we'd write them in a way that we would perform them. So we said fuck it, maybe we'll put a band together and see how it goes.'

Nathan, Caleb, Ken Levitan and Angelo Petraglia subsequently flew to New York where they played for nine labels in two days, the two brothers singing while Petraglia accompanied them on guitar. Out of the nine auditions, they got four offers. One of the execs checking out the Followills was veteran A&R man Steve Ralbovsky, who had done time for companies as diverse as Columbia, A&M, Elektra, and Arista and had worked with such acts as Tom Verlaine, the Red Hot Chili Peppers, Anthrax, the Breeders and Ween. Having joined RCA in 1998, he had successfully nurtured musicians such as David Gray and My Morning Jacket and was the man responsible for signing the Strokes – quite a track record! He certainly had his ears attuned to the right kind of music.

'There was no band, and hardly enough songs for half an album, but there was something incredibly special about the two of them,' Ralbovsky would later recall. He liked what they played him, particularly an irresistible hook-laden tune entitled 'California Waiting', but RCA's initial idea was to team the pair up with a flashy little backing band. That was Nathan and Caleb's cue. 'We were like, Fuck no! We've always been the guys that'll say "Fuck you" first so we called up our cousin Matthew who was at high school in Mississippi and said, "If you want to be in the band you've got to drop out of school and move down here *now*!"' He was so keen to be involved he auditioned for them playing his guitar over the telephone!

Born Cameron Matthew Followill on 10 September 1984, cousin Matthew had listened to rock from an early age, his dad making him tapes of Thin Lizzy's 'Jailbreak' and ZZ Top to play on his Walkman. Academically speaking a no-hoper, Matthew would have probably ended up painting houses like his other male relatives, if a history teacher at school hadn't taken pity on him and offered him classical guitar lessons. 'I loved it', he told *Mojo* proudly, adding that 'I was definitely the best in my class.' By the age of 13 he was stealing electric guitar licks from his beloved Thin Lizzy. 'The solo on "Cowboy Song" is awesome', he reckons, 'and Phil Lynott's voice is so *cool*. He always sang about motorcycles and bars and girls but in the coolest way.'

It all paints a picture of a teenage axe hero in waiting. Yet, funnily enough, Matthew hadn't even played the guitar for four years when he got the call from his cousins! He was much keener on computer games and proved himself to be something of an expert. He wasn't used to losing, either, as he'd later show when he threw a PS3 controller at the wall of his lounge hard enough to make a dent after losing to Jared in a game of Mortal Kombat. His previous jobs, apart from the aforementioned house-painting, included being a runner for a law firm. Neither occupation was likely to buy him his dream machine, a Harley Davidson motorbike, so he was happy enough to get on board.

Then, sensing that their 15-year-old brother Jared wanted to leave school and join as well, Nathan and Caleb hired him as their bass player. Jared needed some

convincing as he confided to *Mojo*. 'I knew the music
I turned Nathan and Caleb on to had influenced their
songwriting style completely, but I felt like there was an
obligation to involve me. Like "We can't fuck him and
leave him there with Mom!"' And the instrument his
brothers wanted him to play didn't much attract him either
– he felt the four-string bass guitar was 'unglamorous'.
But as he told *Mojo* 'with the Strokes, bass lines kind of
made a comeback, so it was perfect timing for me. And
there are some really cool bass players: (the Clash's) Paul
Simonon, (New Order's) Peter Hook….'

As kids, Matthew and Jared were a self-confessed
handful – when they were young, their mothers took them
on a visit to New York. As Matthew later told *Rolling
Stone*, 'We got into *so* much trouble. I was peeing in
elevators, lighting towels and throwing them into the pool.
We were stealing cigars and smoking 'em.' Hellraiser
Matthew even went joyriding: 'I stole the car and I drove
it down the wrong way on to a highway ramp.' But the
highlight of the trip was undoubtedly when he got put
in jail – only for an hour – after he shot an old woman
with a paintball gun. 'When I look back on this stuff, it's
crazy. Was I possessed?' he now quips. It may not quite
have had the ring of the Who or Zeppelin about it, but
it was behaviour that had all the makings of a bad-ass
rock'n'roller in training.

Still interested in their embryonic talent but thrown
for a loop that the Followills wanted to form their own
outfit, Ralbovsky sent them back to Nashville and gave
them time to rehearse and knock the band into shape
before a second audition, little knowing that Jared hadn't
even played bass in his life! He also mailed Nathan a Led
Zeppelin box set as a blueprint for the kind of sound he

had in mind!

The gang withdrew to Betty Ann's house, soaked up the entire Zep repertoire in one hit and set to work honing their sound. For guys who'd never heard much more than 'Stairway To Heaven', it was a real eye-opener. 'We kidnapped our cousin from Mississippi,' Caleb recalls, 'told his Mom he was coming for the week and just never let him go home. We locked ourselves in the basement with an ounce of marijuana and literally spent a month down there. My Mom would bring us food down. And at the end of that month the label people came and we had "Molly's Chambers", "California Waiting", "Wicker Chair" and "Holy Roller Novocaine".'

Nathan considers the Kings fortunate 'to get a record deal where the label was willing to grow with us, let us take our bruises and figure out the kind of band we were and the band we wanted to be. When we signed the deal it was just me and Caleb. The label said, "We're gonna put you a band together", and we were like, "We don't want to be Evan & Jaron. We're gonna buy our little brother a bass, he's a freshman in high school. Caleb will teach himself to play guitar. Our cousin played guitar when he was 10. I'll play the drums, I played in church when I was little." They said, "All right, we'll come down in one month and see you guys."'

By the time Steve Ralbovsky and his team arrived in Mount Juliet, the band had their four 'basement songs' off pat. Legend has it that in the early days they would resort to prayer to calm their nerves before shows. And they almost blew the second audition. 'We still messed up when the time came,' Matthew recounted to *Mojo* magazine, 'but, thank God, they liked what they saw.'

A contract with Elvis Presley's old label, RCA Records,

was finally inked. Straight after they'd signed, Nathan and Caleb went out and bought a car for their grandma and then a house which they purchased from an elderly couple for a 'coupla thousand dollars.' Now all they all they needed was a band name. Angelo Petraglia came up with Kings of Zion, inspired by their religious upbringing – Caleb gave it a quick tweak, substituting Leon, their father and grandfather's name, in place of Zion, and hey presto! One of the biggest rock bands in the history of the twenty-first century was finally in business – in name, at least.

Now came the hard part, getting down to making their first record. There was no better way to tighten up the music than to put it in a live setting, so the newly christened Kings of Leon made their first live appearance opening for the Skeeters and outlaw country star Billie Joe Shaver at Smith's Olde Bar in Atlanta. As Caleb later revealed to *Rolling Stone*, it was one of the scariest moments of his entire life.

'We walked in and saw all the cowboy hats and I literally said to the guys, "You fuckin' country it up. Tonight these songs will be alternative country." And we fuckin' went out there and people were takin' their cowboy hats off goin' "Whooo!" and fuckin' lovin' it, even though we were dressed like (proto-punks) the New York Dolls. When the curtains closed, it was like a *90210* moment – we all gave each other high fives.'

But this was no escapist television programme – this was real life. And Kings of Leon were about to take it by the horns….

CHAPTER THREE

HOLY ROLLERS

The stage was set for the Kings of Leon to make their first recording in 2002. And while they were understandably keen to keep mentor Angelo Petraglia on board, record company RCA brought in a 'safe pair of hands' to work alongside him and oversee the sessions – in the shape of Ethan Johns, the son of legendary British producer Glyn Johns.

Ethan started life as a session musician, playing for and with the likes of the Wallflowers (led by Jakob Dylan, Bob's son), Emmylou Harris/Linda Ronstadt, John Hiatt, Green on Red, Joe Satriani, Stevie Nicks and Crosby Stills and Nash. He then took a step back from being a multi-instrumentalist, preferring to press his claims as a producer, engineer and mixer.

It was a case of like father, like son. Johns senior had made a reputation for himself in the sixties and seventies, working with some of the biggest names in rock on some of their most classic albums – the Beatles, the Stones, the Who, Steve Miller Band, the Faces, Humble Pie and the Eagles. As well as Glyn's achievements, Ethan's Uncle Andy had almost as great a track record, having produced Television's all-time classic *Marquee Moon* as well as working with acts as diverse as Jimi Hendrix, Led Zeppelin, Free and Van Halen. There was clearly something in the family's musical DNA....

Another crucial link was Johns' junior's role in piloting the career of maverick singer-songwriter Ryan Adams. His most notable achievement was Adams' second solo record *Gold* (2001), which had been a major commercial highpoint, while he had more recently produced Rufus Wainwright, Counting Crows and temperamental Aussie rockers the Vines. With that kind of clientele he seemed the perfect candidate to capture the rebellious spirit of the Followills' music.

Ethan had spent his childhood watching his father make records in the traditional manner, and adopted a similar purist approach on every record he made. This could encompass everything from playing the drums on basic tracks and using his own musical talents to overdub numerous additional parts, to making tape edits with a razor.

There were no computers in Johns' studio. He was no fan of digital technology, preferring things to happen in real time and documented on two-inch, 16-track tape. 'I've tried using (digital editing software) ProTools,' he told writer Bud Scoppa, 'but I can't get a balance with digital noise, and it doesn't sound good to my ears. For me there's no reason to use it, because it doesn't do anything as a tool that tape doesn't.'

While ProTools was technically the best editor, Johns didn't like to alter musicians' performances so didn't have a use for that side of the tool. 'Tape helps me get the sound I want to get. It's like having another member of the band, almost, or another engineer. And digital doesn't allow me to do that, so I don't use it.'

Johns' preferred way of working was, to use the age-old cliché, capturing the moment – and that's literally what he did with the Kings. 'If we hit something... and it's the first run-through, and somebody doesn't make the bridge...or we just happen to get a particularly great outro on one take, then I'll cut that into the multi-track with a razorblade and cut the takes together.'

There was plenty of this remedial work to be done in the early stages, as the boys' technical ability was, to say the least, shaky. And that was hardly surprising – after all they'd never really played together in a band context. 'When I met them, they hadn't been playing together for five minutes, but because they were a family they knew how to communicate instinctively,' says their producer. 'They had this fiery energy.'

Talking about those first sessions which would culminate in the band's debut EP, Angelo Petraglia commented: 'Usually I bring down all the guitars to the studio, so we're constantly circulating guitars and amps. On the "Holy Roller Novocaine" EP Matthew used my '71 Les Paul Deluxe Goldtop.'

The Les Paul was and remains the ultimate rock'n'roll guitar, its thick, meaty tones the basis of innumerable rock classics. Slash from Guns N'Roses is a legendary user, as was Eric Clapton in his days with Cream. Led Zeppelin's Jimmy Page and ZZ Top's Billy Gibbons among its many other adherents. Cousin Matthew has relied on the Les Paul ever since, with another Followill cousin Michael – known to one and all as 'Nacho' – taking care of it on and off-stage as the band's roadie.

As for young neophyte Jared, Angelo observed, 'When I initially met him he had never played bass. We bought him a Fender at first, then we went to Gruhn's (music shop) and bought an EB-0. But a Thunderbird is really his choice – he has a bunch of those now. The way the Thunderbird cuts (through) is great for his style of playing.' Both the basses mentioned are made by Gibson – unusually, since the rival Fender company set the standard with their Precision and Jazz Bass designs.

Yet the angular, distinctive Thunderbird, most usually seen toted by Spandex-wearing heavy metallers of the eighties, would become both a visual and aural trademark of both musician and band. Treated and/or distorted bass lines have been, in their own way, as integral to the KoL sound as Caleb's vocals or Matthew's guitar.

Angelo remembers that early in the songwriting process he handed Caleb his precious 1972 Gibson ES-325. He'd found the semi-acoustic rarity on Internet auction site eBay and bought it for a bargain-basement $900! Like Kings of Leon's music, it seemed somewhat older than it actually was. That precious 325 would appear on all the band's subsequent records and was also played on stage until it met a violent death at 2009's T in the Park Festival.

Once they'd sorted out their instruments, there was no stopping the Kings. They hunkered down to recording a bunch of songs, including 'Absent', supposedly about Caleb's childhood sweetheart Marnie Jensen, which was later discarded from the final release. In addition to his role at the controls, Johns played guitar, percussion and Hammond organ while Angelo Petraglia played both electric and acoustic guitars. Petraglia was also credited as co-writer of all the songs along with Caleb and Nathan.

The 'Holy Roller Novocaine' EP was released on 18 February 2003. This was quite a departure for a band from Nashville, boasting a distinctive and different sound. 'Around 2002, Nashville was all country music,' Matthew would later observe. 'There were guys we knew outside of town who played punk music and we would hang out with them. But there was nothing going on.' This was dirty, swampy hard-assed rock'n'roll bulging with attitude but also melodic and not without a radio-friendly sheen.

The 15-minute EP offered up a slice of sincere, blues-tinged, anthemic Tennessee rock that, for all its throwback styling, boasted an exceptionally twenty-first century sound. 'Holy Roller' contained five songs, which mixed late-sixties garage rock with sprawling seventies guitar rock, but the resulting sound was fresh and new enough. And in among the frequent nods to the past – Steppenwolf, the Kinks, Neil Young, the Band etc – you could sense the band's love of the Strokes and other contemporary acts. After all, this was the era of the White Stripes and, after the sterility of the Brit-Pop era, no-nonsense rock'n'roll was back in fashion and in demand.

The bluesy-tinged opener, 'Molly's Chambers', may have sounded like imitation Black Crowes, with a guitar solo straight out of an early Lynyrd Skynyrd album. But the Kings convinced because they delivered it with a youthful enthusiasm that exuded a real air of 'we're so stoked to be playing music'. And the band could rock with the best of them, as the aggressive honky-tonk sound of 'Wasted Time' soon proved. As evinced here, Caleb could effortlessly switch from a warm Southern drawl to a more ferocious whisky-flavoured roar.

For many fans and reviewers, 'California Waiting' was the standout cut on 'Holy Roller', a poppy, catchy piece of jangling sunshine-filled feelgood rock with attractive chiming acoustic guitars and a chorus that was perfect to tap along to on the top of your car dashboard. Powered by Jared's clean, for once undistorted bass and Nathan's propulsive drumming, it led one scribe to compare its melody and feel to one of Mancunian misery merchants New Order's early hits, 'Ceremony'! While the blandest cut on offer, it had an engaging immediacy.

In contrast 'Holy Roller Novocaine's title track was a far more dynamic, raucous affair, characterised by Caleb's lecherous vocals and suggestive lyrics. A number about a preacher taking advantage of the more vulnerable members of his congregation (sound familiar?), full of sexual swagger and bravado, this was the one track that was most representative of the Kings' musical style and sound going forward.

The straight-ahead closer, the country-rock ballad 'Wicker Chair', was arguably the other standout cut on this debut, topped as it was with gentle cymbal strokes and lush acoustic guitar strumming. 'Trey Boyer would play guitar while me and Nate sang,' Caleb recalled to *Rolling Stone* magazine. 'One day he taught me a C chord, and that night I was playing it and Jared came downstairs and sat in our white wicker chair. When Nathan wasn't looking, I'd get stoned with Jared and we'd have a good time. So I remember writing the opening lyrics about Jared "in your little white wicker chair, unsuspicious?" And then I wrote the rest of the song about my dad.'

Interestingly 'Wicker Chair' would the one and only song from the 'Holy Roller Novocaine' EP that didn't make it to the first album in one form or another. Perhaps the brothers felt it couldn't be improved upon, or maybe they just wanted to include more new music. It stayed firmly on the live set list for some while, however, and a rousing version from the Roskilde Festival in 2004 was made available as B-side to 'The Bucket' single later that year.

Manager Levitan would later admit that the game plan was to break the band overseas first, partly because of the chance that Americans weren't ready for a Nashville-based rock band, and partly because of ongoing staff changes at RCA in the States. 'We tried to break it out of Europe first. We thought they really might get the music and the story quicker there than they did here,' Levitan says. 'So basically we hopped on a plane, got the guys over, hired a publicist, got the label fired up and away it went.'

And the plan worked to perfection. The British music press, particularly market leader the *New Musical Express*, were quick to embrace these Southern boys with their hair, a couple of moustaches and beards and super-tight jeans.

Out in cyberspace, the *Music OMH* website was one of many that waxed lyrical: 'Every once in a while a band creeps up and makes people sit up. I mean sit up, with pupils dilated, ears attuned and mouth moistening. Kings of Leon are exactly that type of band. And this debut EP is a little sampler of the promising talent which exists in the secluded Deep American South.'

Ireland's CLUAS website also approved: 'The vocals are deep and half high-school geeky but make an impression pretty quickly. "Molly's Chambers" isn't as strong a tune as it at first promises to be. Swerving back and over the highway, the pedal only goes down on this machine in the second half of the song, with fleshy guitars and a hooky beat. Far better is the next song up, the more laid back and less stilted "California Waiting". "Can I get back my lonely life?" is Caleb's plaintive cry as guitars chug along and a soft drum focus build the tune up to something utterly likeable.' They concluded accurately that 'They've got the look, they're no slouches in serving up some delectable guitars so Kings of Leon could do quite well for themselves.'

After testing the waters with their debut EP, the Kings were ready to record their debut album, and this was already eagerly anticipated by critics. The boys headed to California and Sound City Studios, with that end in mind. They were in good company, with Nirvana's *Nevermind* having been recorded there 12 years previously. The Kings were already making statements. They were prepared to fill the rock footsteps ahead of them, and the production team of Johns and Petraglia was already in place.

Recording was split with the Shangri-La Studio in nearby Malibu. Once inhabited by the Band, Bob Dylan's backing group, it was sacred territory for the boys. 'Every interview that was filmed (for *The Last Waltz* movie) was filmed in Shangri-La!' says Matthew, in obvious awe of his idols. 'That's where we recorded the new album. That band built it! We were in the halls [where] they recorded. It was like a museum, we didn't want to touch anything, fuck anything up.'

With rumours also abounding that the studio was once used as a 'brothel to the stars' many years ago, the theme of debauchery and depravity sat well with the band, who were rapidly garnering a reputation of enjoying a party or three. Caleb told *NME*: 'We're not naturally bad persons; we're fairly considerate people. But occasionally you have to go a bit crazy; otherwise you're fucked from the pressure. Sometimes you just have to act like a kid.' Nathan added, 'It's not like we're trying to be these party animals or the most fucked-up band in town or whatever.'

The pressure certainly didn't appear to phase the Followills – which was just as well, as in the run-up to the LP's release the Kings found themselves very much in demand on the European live scene. The band first hit the United Kingdom at the beginning of 2003 when they were invited to London in February to appear at the *New Musical Express* annual awards. They were holed up in the infamous Columbia Hotel, a rock'n'roll watering hole from which Oasis's Gallagher Brothers among others had been banned.

Caleb couldn't believe the scenes of debauchery unfolding around them, with ne'er an eyebrow raised. 'The first couple of nights,' he said, 'we were sitting there just looking around laughing. It was like a movie, but worse. It was absolutely, completely crazy, like a damn circus.' He told tales of people snorting drugs off tables, throwing champagne bottles and worse... and when the band got back to their home country they chronicled the trip in the song 'Spiral Staircase'. Their eyes had been opened for better or worse, and they would eventually embrace the oh-so-enjoyable excesses of the rock'n'roll lifestyle they had witnessed.

Back in the States, the task of recording the album awaited. Caleb revealed the band's attitude was not regimented, rather an organic process moulded from song to song. 'In our record-making process we kinda move around a little bit, and wherever we are we try to record a little here and a little there.' Recording at Shangri-La was 'a great experience. Every song is different; some of the songs we would record with not even the headphones on – just looking at each other. We can't even really hear it, we're just playing together.'

It was this philosophy of treating every song like a disparate, different entity that Caleb suggested made the band different. Despite their appearance and subsequent pigeonholing, the Followills claimed they weren't tied down to a specific genre. 'We have so many different influences,' Caleb told Zane Lowe on MTV UK's *Gonzo* show. 'Some influences are about the music, some are about the songwriting, every kind of music, every genre. We try not to hold ourselves down to anything; we try not to put a genre on us. It's about the songs; song to song, whatever they require….'

So why exactly were the Kings so immediately popular with British audiences? According to Gareth Grundy, deputy editor of British music magazine *Q*, when Kings of Leon arrived in the wake of the Strokes and White Stripes, 'suddenly every pretty American boy with interesting hair, tight jeans and Chuck Taylors was selling out big shows in London. Britain has a history of embracing and occasionally breaking esoteric American bands first. I'm thinking of anything from the Pixies to the White Stripes and, more recently, the Killers, whose album seems to have tenure in the Top 5 here. There remains a huge appetite for new music over here, and the current UK mainstream - made up of Franz Ferdinand, Scissor Sisters and the Killers as much as Green Day and U2 - probably looks left-field to the average US music fan.'

"I think our story was romanticized in Europe,' agrees Jared. "Our first record is a great record when you think about everything that comes along with it: how we look, where we came from, all the stuff with our father. In England, they put it all into perspective. But in America, it was different. The South is kind of looked down upon, and people didn't really know anything about us here, they just heard this raw music. America tends to be into big productions and hip-hop, and our music is pretty much the opposite of that.'

The UK media were indeed abuzz with the Kings' back-story and their unkempt Southern look. Indeed, everything described in relation to the band had to be Southern; particularly when in comparison with fellow American band the Strokes. 'The Southern Strokes' was a description that would follow the boys round for the next few years.

Nathan was understandably quick to tire of the comparisons to Julian Casablancas and co. 'It's like when Nirvana came out – every band that came out after was a rip-off of them, be it Pearl Jam or whoever, so in every area you're gonna have that one band that opens the door, and everybody else is gonna be riding their coat tails.' But he put a brave face on things. 'It doesn't bother us at all. We play totally different music to the Strokes, the only similarity is we all have dicks and long hair!'

Far from shirking from their roots, the band embraced them – as long as it was in the right spirit. 'We're proud of our heritage. Where we come from tends to have a stigma, all that Lynyrd Skynyrd shit. But, you know, there's Johnny Cash too. We're just happy making good music and having fun,' Caleb told *GQ* magazine.

The Kings were happy, yet keen not to be over-exposed; the album hadn't dropped yet, and critical attention, especially without music to back it up, could have its pros and cons. The band no longer jumped at every opportunity for an interview or a photo shoot, as Caleb explained: 'It's something at this point we've never really had to worry about, not now it's getting to the point where we can be a little more selective. I just don't want people to get tired of us, and tired of hearing "the story".'

He recognized it was the boys' background that helped distinguish them from other bands emerging at the same time, but believed it was the music that would set them apart further still. 'I think that we're honest enough with ourselves to know that at first a lot of the hype was about our story, and about the fact that we're family, and our dad and stuff, but once people got to meet us they realised we're actually a good band. It's not all about that.' With the album ready for release, the band was hoping their image and biography would become secondary.

The album finally hit the racks on 7 July in the UK, a month later in the US, and featured versions of four out of the five tracks on 'Holy Roller Novocaine', with only 'Wicker Chair' missing the cut. The album's title provoked speculation as to its origins, with some believing it was taken from Ernest Hemingway's memoirs *A Moveable Feast*, but Caleb revealed it was straight out of their father's preaching past. 'We were going through a box of all kinds of old stuff, and we found my Dad's old preaching bible. There was this cool-looking tree in the back of it called the Tree of Life, and on each branch it said something different. One of them was 'youth and young manhood.' The album title says a lot about us and our band, where we are and the things that we're going through.'

Nathan warned prospective listeners of what to expect from the band who, by now, were whipping up significant critical kudos: 'We're beautiful and raw; we're not polished musicians, we're not studio cats, what you see is what you get – no façade, no nothing. I mean, damn – that's it!'

Caleb felt the raw sound contributed to the album's

quick recording and release. 'It seems like everything we do comes together really quickly. It might not seem like it but it really does, like our recording process – we're pretty easy to work with because we don't like to sound too good! We wanna sound good, but not *too* good!'

The LP certainly backed that up; it was an unpolished and gritty expression of the band's experiences and those around them to date and with 12 tracks squeezed into just 40 minutes, it mirrored how those experiences had been crammed in to just a few short years. As *New Musical Express* breathlessly put it, 'This is not a chirpy, good-time romp…rather, the Kings hold up a mirror to the messier side of their childhood.'

Nathan paid tribute to the part played by Ethan Johns. 'He let us keep it as raw as we wanted it, while still keeping it within the boundaries of a record that sounds great. He was very patient with us, very understanding. He just got the songs; he was in it from day one. The first demos we heard he was ready to go. He just basically let us be as natural as we could be, and just played off that. We got awesome sounds. Awesome guitar sounds, awesome drum sounds. He was definitely the man for the job. And we definitely couldn't have made a better first record!'

Youth And Young Manhood was guaranteed to be an explosive ride. It kicked off with 'Red Morning Light', opening with Matthew's arresting guitar riff before Caleb bounds in with his rhythm guitar and trademark croak. Raunchily singing 'You always like it under covers/Tucked in between your dirty little sheets', it was clear from the outset these weren't lyrics for the easily offended.

And that included Betty Ann, their beloved mother. Interestingly, Jared revealed that the Kings' salacious songs lyrics had reduced her to tears. 'My Mom can never really understand the lyrics so when I tell her about them she gets so sad… So I tell her to think of it as like a movie or something.'

As if the 'Holy Roller Novocaine' EP hadn't been indication enough, 'Red Morning Light' launched an album whose subject matter was to be anything but run of the mill. As Nathan told *NME*: 'All that most music really is right now is crappy fairy tale songs about boy-girl or love or whatever. We'd rather put ourselves in the shoes of some of the people we've encountered. We don't necessarily feel the same way as some of the people in the songs, but I guess that you just have to try and take yourself to that place.'

Track two, 'Happy Alone', doesn't let you catch your breath. Matthew and Caleb once again combine their guitars and send you frantically through four minutes of pure whiskey-saturated Southern rock, while Nathan's drumming makes you wonder how he can keep that speed up for the duration without his arms falling off. The aim, Caleb said, was to create an album 'like a good movie soundtrack. I want it to have everything in it, all parts of life.'

A different version of 'Wasted Time' than was heard on the 'Holy Roller' EP was up next, and was the album's second single, charting at UK Number 51 in October 2003. The track, which 'justified their reputation as "The Southern Strokes", according to one critic, featured Jared's bass getting some exposure as Caleb murmurs 'time on me is wasted time' – the Kings had arrived, and they ain't no good!

'Joe's Head' offers a change of pace after the album's whirlwind opening statement of intent. It has been described by some as a ballad, but in reality is far from it. While the track in truth is not a highlight, it would clearly be a festival favourite with its jaunty, dancealong pace. Once more the lyrical content was nothing if not controversial – a man catches his girlfriend cheating, so he kills them both, Caleb singing matter-of-factly of the killer's next action 'Then he lit up a cigarette' – what would the church think?

But the Kings were prepared to push the envelope further with their next track. Not only was this to become a cult favourite, but it would even be singled out for praise by rock godfather Bob Dylan in the future. 'Trani', as the name suggests, depicted the story of a fallen transvestite high on cocaine. The song was a sign of versatility for the band, the pace slowed almost to a halt and the track building up over five minutes – the longest on the album. There was clearly more to the Kings than barnburners and themes for hoe-downs. However it came as no surprise when Caleb admitted, 'our family have learned to listen to our music selectively.'

A re-recorded 'California Waiting' was up next. This offered another opportunity for Jared to showcase his bass, although sadly drowned out again by his brothers and cousin. The balance between the instruments would be something that would change as the band's music progressed. The track's anthemic chorus made it the perfect choice for the third single from the album. Released in February 2004, it reached Number 61 in the UK but did not chart in the band's native United States.

As previously noted, 'Spiral Staircase' was said to be about the Kings' experiences when landing in Britain for the first time. As Caleb recalled, 'It was like, "What the fuck?!" People were snorting coke off the tables, pissing and puking out the windows... It was absolutely, completely crazy.'

These times are reflected in a frenetic track reminiscent of the Libertines in their pomp, screeching in at under three minutes with Caleb's off-key whining adding to the sense of hazy confusion. *NME* described it as 'A saloon-bar brawl between the riff from the Stones' "Satisfaction" and "Bob Dylan's 115th Dream".'

Most recording artists tend to pile their most immediate tracks towards the top of the running order, for fear potential purchasers will fail to show persistence. Not this group! Track eight of the album would, against the odds, become Kings of Leon's first career standout single. The album's shortest track at just over two minutes, 'Molly's Chambers' sees Jared coming into his own. The bass line he created provides the driving force behind the track, which was inspired by a line in Thin Lizzy's take on the traditional Irish song 'Whiskey In The Jar'.

It became the first single released from the album, and reached Number 23 in the UK charts in August 2003. For years to come it would be the outstanding dance number in the Kings' sets, popular with both old and new fans alike. It also attracted cover versions and became something of a bar-band staple.

It also inspired Kings of Leon's debut video, a low-key affair that would set the style for all the band's videos to come. Predominantly performance-based, it simply showed the Kings playing in a black room intermittently doused in splashes of psychedelic colour. It was largely unimpressive but showed the boys were focused on the music rather than the ancillary add-ons designed to get a band noticed.

The visual accompaniment to follow-up single 'Wasted Time' took the band out of the studio and into a drug-fuelled wooded field, with multiple extras – including half-naked women dancing hedonistically with erratic camera cuts and angles. The Kings had come on by leaps and bounds production-wise but had not strayed from their performance ethos.

The album showed no signs of slowing down as it entered its final third. 'Genius' – perhaps due to its placing in the wake of its radio-friendly neighbour –was largely underrated in subsequent reviews of the album. It's a solid rock track, with a strapping drumbeat and tidy guitar hooks.

The Kings then embarked on the barren Wild West expanse of 'Dusty', bringing the tempo right down and showing they could dictate the pace and produce a convincing display of different emotions. The quartet were not to be limited to frenetic two-minute stormers, great though they were. 'A lot of people have a lot of fast songs on their CD, or all slow songs,' commented Matthew. 'Like the Rolling Stones, they almost have more slow songs than upbeat ones. So we just even it out.'

The penultimate track was already well known. 'Holy Roller Novocaine'; the title cut from their first EP, set the scene for the album closer. 'Talihina Sky' was inspired by the boys' visits to the annual Followill family reunions in Talihina, Oklahoma. This unannounced 'hidden track' was a homage to their relatives, most of whom would never experience the life of Kings – a state of affairs not lost on Caleb.

The album was a solid debut by any yardstick and announced the boys' arrival to the waiting world. They had managed to juggle the recording of their first album with cramming in a decade of missed teen years, and done a good job. But that was no surprise to Caleb. 'I don't like to go through all the bullshit clichés of rock'n'roll, sitting here and talking about all the things we do. We have our good times, and sometimes it gets in the way of working, but for the most part we hold it down when we have to hold it down.'

On the face of it, there was a lot of dark subject-matter for listeners to digest in the likes of 'Trani', 'Joe's Head', 'Red Morning Light' and 'Spiral Staircase' – the Kings covering transvestism, murders, prostitutes and orgies in the space of just four songs – but the whole thing was carried off with youthful aplomb. *New Musical Express*, the British music paper that would consistently champion their cause, was happy to acclaim *Youth And Young Manhood* 'The Album of 2003'. It was, they said, 'a record that does for hoary old country rock what the Strokes did for pasty New York new wave, taking the pipe'n'slippers former listening option of people who get excited about hairy old bands and adding laser-sighted choruses, indie cred, sex appeal and, above all, fun.'

Indeed, they put it up on a pedestal alongside stellar opening shots *Is This It* (the Strokes) and *Definitely Maybe* (Oasis), proclaiming it 'one of the most exciting debut albums of the last few years.' Indeed, 'the Kings were to 2003 what Oasis were to 1994 and the Strokes were to 2001 – the most exciting new rock band of the year.' A Number 3 chart position confirmed the hype was justified.

Many critics were making comparisons with the Strokes, which inspired an internet reviewer using the screen name 'Wheelchair Assassin' to pen the following mixture of indignation and finely tuned analysis: 'The Strokes could take a few lessons from these guys. Instead of retro urban cool, the Kings offer a booze-fuelled good time, equal parts rootsy and rocking, that should have plenty of appeal for rock fans seeking a legitimate alternative to the prevailing trends of the day.

'While I didn't hear any echoes of the Strokes here, that's not to say these guys don't remind me of anyone else, but you have to reach back a little further in rock history to find some parallels. If anything, their occasionally incendiary, slapped-together, southern-accented sound makes me think of the Replacements or Dinosaur Jr cross-bred with Creedence Clearwater Revival. The Kings specialize in up-tempo rockers filled with screaming guitars and hard-driving rhythms, topped off by the garbled drawl of singer Caleb Followill. Showing a grasp of dynamics to rival the mighty Pixies, the songs often pick up steam early on before shifting into overdrive for some of the most insanely catchy choruses in recent memory. And the guitar solos are models of efficiency, accomplishing more in a few seconds than you might think possible.'

Another blogger, Adrian Denning, reiterated the point that while so many albums 'pack the first half with great songs and leave the second to fend for itself, *Youth And Young Manhood* gets better and better as it goes along. Clever stuff, stick your best songs near the end so people remember their seventies experience with a happy smile… They may have stepped right out of the then but their guitar player at least has lived through the eighties and nineties and it shows… The Kings of Leon understand the value of a simple guitar line that's easy to hum.'

There were, of course, dissenters in the ranks. *Popmatters* website pointed a finger at the songwriting in particular. 'The Strokes, even if they are such gifted recyclers…can at least write a damn catchy song. Kings of Leon, on the other hand, imbues its performances with an admirable jolt of energy, but the songs are so generic that the only thing left at the record's conclusion is the feeling of how hollow and insubstantial the whole thing is.

'There are a couple of exceptions in the record's first half—"Trani" (which is really nothing more than a slowed-down "Sweet Jane" with Mick Jagger's "Far Away Eyes" vocal thrown over the top) and the genuine pop single "California Waiting"—but the rest is virtually unmemorable, unless the "Nirvana with no soul" rave-up "Molly's Chambers" or the fact that they can play a waltz ("Dusty") can be considered return-worthy traits.'

The similarly sceptical *Sputnik Music* site likened Kings of Leon to 'Lynard Skynard (sic) with an iPod. They're basically a modern-day Country Blues act. There's no real progression in their sound and there lyrics are often unbearable yet they've sold a ton of records and get the *NME* seal of approval.' The 'Blues-tinged Country Rock sound you've heard a million times over' could, they said, be 'the Rolling Stones without the swagger or attitude or the Who after too much Moon Shine.' And Caleb's vocals are 'bland and lazy with the often outburst of demented howling and confused rambling... they lack intent and thought and sound like they could be sung by a 40-year-old Pub singer.'

For his part, Caleb was unlikely to be swayed by either hyperbolic praise or pessimistic panning, no matter from which source it emanated. He was already looking forward to the next recording sessions. 'Hopefully we can release another record sometime soon – we would like to, but our record was released in America later, so it's still doing things there. But we're very excited about it, we think it's the greatest thing we've ever done, and I don't know what the rest of the world will think, but before this record we didn't have any fans, so we only made that for ourselves, and we're not gonna change the way we make music.'

The Kings' first tour of Britain saw them acclaimed as the conquering heroes the music press had proclaimed them to be. The Electric Ballroom in London's trendy Camden was crammed with wall-to-wall celebrities, with actress Sadie Frost, Beatle brat/clothes designer Stella McCartney and supermodel Kate Moss seen queuing for a backstage dressing-room audience with the new kids on the block.

Not that every show would be that dramatic. Back in February the Kings had warmed up for their *NME* awards show appearance in a pub in rural High Wycombe, north of London, playing support to an audience of less than 200, and some of the summer shows were in venues that were not that much bigger. The reaction of four Nashville cats to the earthy seaside delights of Scarborough, for instance, was fascinating, but Scarborough's reaction to them, far from being reserved Yorkshire, was ecstatic. Lenswoman Jo McCaughey, who accompanied them on the tour, said 'they were unaware of how popular they were...it didn't phase them, it was normal.'

The Kings merely thought this was what happened when you were in a band. And so far at least nothing had happened to cloud their rose-tinted spectacles. But off stage they were already ready to dive headlong into the rock'n'roll lifestyle. And remember that two members of the band, Matthew and Jared, were still too young to legally consume alcohol in their native United States.

For the ever-thirsty Matthew in particular, coming to England was 'awesome. We'd play the show and immediately start drinking beer.' But drugs were something else again... and not always knowingly ingested. One night Caleb found out someone had given some really strong ecstasy. The rest of the band found him behind a PA speaker. 'It was the loudest music ever and I had a huge smile and tears pouring out of my eyes. I was crying and enjoying it at the same time.'

The Kings also admitted they used to take advantage of groupies and even had fights over who was going to bed the best-looking girl. "One of the perks of being in this band,' said Nathan, 'is that 80 per cent of our crowd are girls. We're super-competitive so after a show, if your girl's prettier than my girl, I'm going to try to take your girl from you. We had gotten our first taste of the benefits of the lifestyle, for sure.'

The family's itinerant lifestyle as children had clearly helped them adapt to the transitory nature of life on the rock'n'roll road. 'I think it was awesome that we got to see the whole United States growing up,' said Nathan, looking back. 'Of course we missed out on having the same friends for three years in school, or graduating with buddies who we've known for so long. But it was pretty much a week: meet them on Monday, best friends by Tuesday, and sad when you have to leave on Friday. But obviously, life on the road definitely prepared us for this.'

The Followills killed time between dates on the tour bus playing cards and drinking coffee, like most regular bands would. With their cousin a guitar roadie, there was very much a family feel about the whole organisation, with everybody looking out for each other. This was probably the glue that bound the Kings of Leon operation together, no matter how much the booze and drugs, stresses and strains threatened its integrity.

The Kings' off-stage excesses might have been fun – but it was their on-stage performances that would win them a last-minute invitation to play the Glastonbury Festival.

Their status meant they would be 'slumming it' in the New Bands Tent, but as seasoned Glasto-goers will know that's where the tastemakers hang out ready to acclaim the 'next big thing'. Again, the celebrity fans were out in force, with Noel Gallagher rubbing shoulders with members of the Thrills, the Doves, Primal Scream and Travis, as the boys strutted their Deep-Southern stuff in the deep south-west.

No-one there present would have realised it was the band's first ever festival performance, but five years later when they headlined the event's Pyramid Stage, Caleb revealed it had made a permanent mark on him. 'Right everybody, I don't normally talk a lot but seeing as it's a special occasion I thought I better say a few things,' he explained. 'In June 2003 our band had the honour of playing its first festival, it so happened to be Glastonbury and we've worked our way up to where we are now. Here's to you guys, thanks for letting us do this.' It was followed by another prestigious festival, Scotland's T In The Park, where they pitched up in the New Band Tent to turn in a rip-roaring set. Again, it was a portent of things to come and the preliminary to a headlining appearance six years later.

But returning to 2003, there was little chance the Kings were about to rest on their recently-won laurels. 'We already have six songs written for the second album,' Caleb told *New Musical Express* that summer. 'We want to keep on making music and having a really good time while we have the opportunity. Because pretty soon fashion will turn against us again and no-one will care any more.'

As prophecies go, that was scarcely in the Biblical class…

CHAPTER FOUR

SHAKING HEARTBREAK

For many bands the pressure would be well and truly on to produce a second album that surpassed the first – but not for Kings of Leon, when they returned to the studio in spring 2004. While the Kings were particularly popular with the critics, *Youth And Young Manhood* was also a great commercial triumph, illustrated by the album's success in the UK album charts, peaking at Number 3 and becoming a fixture in the Top 10 for over ten weeks. The second attempt at success in any field is generally considered the hardest, and the band did not want to be remembered as a flash in the pan – so failure was not an option.

They stuck to their winning formula, retaining close friend and production maestro Angelo Petraglia and studio wizard Ethan Johns, and selecting the latter's Three Crows Studio in Los Angeles as the location for laying down the foundations of their sophomore effort. Matthew told of the ease with which the band returned to the recording process. 'We told the label that we were ready to record, they wanted us to and were like "Yeah, let's do it". So we went to LA and caught up with Ethan and just started from there. It took us about six weeks.'

The result would be *Aha Shake Heartbreak*. The title was taken from a track on the album, 'Taper Jean Girl', though Caleb stated, 'It was originally a title for one of the songs off the record and we kinda like the way it rolled off the tongue – or off our tongues, everyone else has trouble with it! We like how it feels, and we think it's how we feel as a band on the second record. We kinda had a lot of time to go out there (for the first album) and have a whirlwind, crazy, blurry couple of moments, and after we had the chance to go home, rest up and relax, we realised what had gone on. It's kinda like the heartbreak after the tornado.'

He revealed that it was the media's focus on the Kings' antics away from the studio that inspired them to return as soon as possible. 'We used to party a lot, and it was enjoyable, but suddenly that was what we became known for. It bugged the hell out of us then and it still does now. Famous people started coming to our shows and that's all anyone would talk about. It made us so mad. We had all this stuff boiling inside us. That's why it was really, really important for us to make another record as soon as possible.'

The experiences from the past 18 months of the boys' lives inevitably found their way into the songs, producing a set of memoirs of the Followills' life of depravity. 'On our first album,' Nathan told *NME*, 'I'd say about 30 per cent of what we were writing about was autobiographical and 70 per cent was wishful thinking. We were writing about things we hadn't seen yet. On this album at least 90 per cent of what we're writing about is things we've experienced, nights we've had. There's still that other ten per cent, though....'

The band had actually been planning to take a break rather than pushing on after a year of continuous touring. 'We really just wanted some time off,' Caleb recalled, 'so we told our management that we weren't going to do anything for two months. But it was really surprising how much we had pent up inside of us from having been on the road and being in each others' hair, that after two weeks we pretty much had enough material to [the point] where we knew we wanted to take the remaining month and go and record.'

The haste with which the band re-entered the studio eliminated any potential second-album pressure and fear of the 'sophomore slump', though Matthew claimed the fear wasn't there. 'The first record we had our whole lives to write. The second one just kinda came to us; it wasn't really hard, it just kinda happened. Most bands would get nervous, but we didn't get the chance to think about it really.'

Jared agreed, claiming it was the band's drive to top what had gone before that played a large part in the process. 'It was more motivation, hearing other people's albums that we liked. When we wrote [*Youth And Young Manhood*] we were really young and we knew we could do better than that, and so we didn't want to sit on it for three years and have that define our band. It was more motivation than pressure to make something better.'

The fact that Kings of Leon were so keen to record a new album – entering the studio less than a year after the release of *Youth And Young Manhood* – raised eyebrows among many. But their blue-collar work ethic would be something the band would become known for in future years. 'We were at home for one month and already going crazy because we weren't used to it' Caleb told the BBC.

'So we ended up writing the record pretty quick, and RCA or BMG or no-one was prepared for us to be ready with another album. We might not be a band that's around for 20 years – we might just make ten really good records in five years.'

It was, perhaps, because the record label weren't ready for such a quick return to the studio by the Followills that, despite recording having finished in June 2004, it would be a further five months before the album appeared in the UK. The US release came later still, in February 2005. The recording process was quick and unrestricted, Caleb revealing that 'once we got (to LA) we'd been rehearsing so much, we talked to Ethan and we realised we wanted to try and record it live as much as possible.' The whole album was recorded as played. 'There was no vocal booth. There was a microphone in the middle of the room and all of us standing around playing and singing. So it's very much like our live show when we're playing real good.

'We just want our music to be as simple,' Caleb continued, 'as far as the way that we record it and play it – as simple as we can, to where there's nothing but us – it's that vulnerable.' So vulnerable, in fact, that it seemed no subject was off limits – including family. 'We wanted this record to be like an open wound. We wanted it to be completely honest and pure. Every one of these songs is about us. They're often blurry memories patched together into a story, but they're about us the whole time. For instance, I wrote "Razz" about Jared because when we were touring he was really pissing me off at times. I just thought there was no point in being anything other than completely honest on this album....'

This honesty transcended the lyrics, and the organic,

live way the album was recorded added to its appeal –
though Caleb was cautious not to appear over-confident.
'There are flaws on this record that we couldn't fix,
because of the way we recorded it. They stay there or you
record it all over again, so we were like, "Well, fuck it."
And now those flaws are beautiful to us. I hope the way
we talk about it doesn't come across as cocky – we're just
really excited.'

Beauty featured on their album cover in the shape of
an incredibly detailed picture of a flower in bloom. 'We
knew we wanted to go with flowers in some way,' said
Caleb. 'We had an amazing photographer go and shoot
a bunch of different flowers and we wanted them shot
in a certain way – in their purest form. We had a lot of
pictures that were really breathtaking, and the album
cover just happened to be one of them. It was really hard
to decide....' So hard, in fact, that the band produced two
album covers. Everything was now set to unleash the new
album on the public.

But the boys would have to wait to show the world
their new brainchild, as the festival season had arrived.
The unquestioned highlight was Glastonbury where, after
debuting a mere 12 months earlier, the Kings were now
warming the crowd up for Oasis, as second on the bill. It
was a different experience from playing the considerably
smaller new bands tent a year prior, as Caleb remembered.
'It was our first festival on the festival tour, so we were
literally *shaking*. It was a huge crowd, but a real honour
to be able to play when we played, and everyone seems
to say we played better than we thought we did.'

He also recalled his encounter with the Gallagher
brothers, Noel and Liam, backstage. 'We gave them some
tips – we heard they were wanting to break into the music

scene, I showed them a couple of licks…' Joking? Perhaps, but even so, the Kings would overtake their Mancunian rivals in just a few short years.

Speaking at the festival, Nathan took a slight jab at his home country, the first rumblings of discontent among the Kings that America had not welcomed one of their own they way Europe had. When asked the difference between crowds at European and American festivals, he replied: 'There are about 95,000 more here then there'd be at an American festival. I just think people in Europe – the UK especially – get cool music easier. America thinks something's cool after everyone else thinks it's cool. Here people like music because they like it.'

Caleb agreed. '[The UK] has their eye on things a little quicker, America… a year and a half later they'll get it. They really have to be spoon-fed what's cool.' The band was keen to break the motherland and become the stars they were across the pond. He was confident success would come – but for now he just wanted to release the album, still a couple of months away, regardless of fans' opinions. 'They can think it's a pile of shit, but we know how proud we are, and we just wanna tell the world we got a secret.'

With so much time elapsing between the completion of recording and release, coupled with the amount of emotion invested in the record by the Followills, a positive reception was paramount. Leading up to the record's release, *NME* enthused: 'You thought you knew Leon's boys? Think again. Second impressions are always more accurate than the first ones. There's more to these ludicrously skinny young men than first meets the eye.'

That second impression came on 1 November in the UK, when *Aha Shake Heartbreak* was released, matching its predecessor by reaching Number 3 in the charts. Lead single 'The Bucket' had arrived a week earlier, complete with music video depicting Caleb *sans* trademark beard and with fashionably straightened hair. 'It was a new album; I had to change a little bit,' he said. 'I actually just took a bath – it was really dirt and it just washed off. Beer foam and dirt!'

The video itself was simple, the band playing live in a makeshift studio with their performance captured through four separate cameras. It reflected the band's honest playing style, a fact Caleb felt was important. 'We were really proud of the way we recorded this record, the fact that we recorded it all live, when it came time to do a video we wanted it to be as close to the way we recorded it as possible. So even though this isn't really a studio, we don't feel like we're playing for cameras or anything like that.'

He explained the idea behind the video in more detail. 'It's pretty much about a lot of stuff that goes on, on the road, this is kinda from the tour manager's perspective – of course we could never have a tour manager!' Jared expressed his pleasure at the performance-based aspect of the three-minute clip. 'You can rock a lot harder than when you actually play because you're not really playing!' 'The Bucket' hit Number 16 on its release, becoming Kings of Leon's highest-charting UK single to date. It was the perfect track to whet the collective appetite of the Followill faithful.

Jared warned that, while the Kings' first album was one to enjoy and celebrate, it was almost a false start for the band. 'To us, this doesn't feel like our second record, it fees like the way our first should have been. We know that with our third record we'll up the stakes a bit more, and hopefully we'll do that with every record.'

The album's first track, 'Slow Night, So Long', set the scene with its 40-second instrumental introduction. Caleb launches into an attack on an unnamed girl he sleeps with despite his low opinion of her; it was also said to have been inspired by his love-hate relationship with Jared's ex-girlfriend. Regardless of the track's origins, lines such as 'You're not so nice but the sex sells so cheap' showed the Kings were back with their no-holds-barred lyrics and no taboo subjects. A calypso-esque shift towards the end showed that they weren't afraid to mix things up musically this time around.

This led on to 'King of The Rodeo', a track described by *NME* as 'a bursting mix of sweat and sand under a desert sky of chiming guitars'. This was released as the third single in April 2005, reaching Number 41. The somewhat literal video saw the band become more creative, with them playing in front of a mass of rodeo revellers performing a choreographed line dance. Jared told *CD:UK* that the video was loosely based on real-life experience: 'The idea for the video kinda came from the first show we played together as a band. We opened for two country acts – the Skeeters and Billy Joe Shaver – and the drummer for the Skeeters really loved us. You could tell he didn't wanna be in a country band any more, he wanted to be in a rock'n'roll band, but he still had his cowboy hat and he was out there dancing, doing his little do-si-do, wrapping his arms around all the girls.'

The album title-inspiring 'Taper Jean Girl' featured guitar-laden verses that sounded like the Kings of old, the track whipping up into a frenzy for the final 30 seconds. A solid effort, but not the highlight of the album by any means. 'Pistol Of Fire' was largely the same; a fast-paced slice of rock'n'roll with a standout guitar solo. Crashing in at a short two minutes 20 seconds, it did not fully illustrate the new direction the Kings were taking.

The band were evolving their sound on this album, and this showed much more on 'Milk'. Starting with the faint pluck of an acoustic guitar, the track focuses on Caleb and his vocal range as he releases an almost primal wail that never once wavers from the note. At four minutes long, it supported the view that the Kings were just as, if not more, effective over a long period of time, than if they tried to compress their frenzied Southern rock into two-minute bursts.

Caleb's high vocal standard on the album could have been attributed to his dropping of certain vices. 'I quit smoking cigarettes for the album. I feel good, but I would like a cigarette. We wrote this one song and it's pretty high, but I really just loved the song. And one day I had a little trouble singing it. I've smoked forever and I've never really had trouble singing. But I decided I liked the song better than I liked cigarettes, so I quit.'

The album reached its halfway point with monster single 'The Bucket'. From Caleb's intro on his rhythm guitar to Nathan crashing in on drums, the song was made for radio. Reportedly written about Jared's introduction to fame at such an early age, with the telling lyrics '18, balding, star', Caleb only went as far as saying, 'it's just a song about it all getting to you and you change into a different person and not really liking the person that you've become.' The song would fit with the Kings' jaded views on the frivolous side of fame. The choice to use it as the album's lead single was not an easy one, as the Kings saw individual releases as ways to advertise what the band is about. 'It's always hard for us to pick singles, because we always want to pick the single that does something to us but it might not necessarily do something for the fan. Also, due to the singles that we've had and due to the press that we've received, people have a preconceived notion of what we are as a band; they expect us to come out with something that's hard-rocking, talking about tobacco chewing and all that stuff. So we kinda wanted to go with the opposite. This record is a lot more about emotions we were feeling on the road, and so hopefully in our single selection we'll be able to capture a lot of different emotions.'

'Soft' would indulge the band's carnal instincts, with Caleb's writing racier and more explicit than perhaps any previous efforts. Caleb left no one in any doubt as to the song's subject matter when he told *Rolling Stone* 'If all people want to talk about is "The Kings of Leon do drugs and hang out with models," I'm gonna give it to them straight. You want to talk about how you saw me doing blow with such-and-such a supermodel? Well you know what my rebuttal is gonna be? "I couldn't get my dick hard that night."'

The brutal honesty in the lyrics and the music was what endeared the band to so many of their fans in the first place. The experiences written into *Aha Shake Heartbreak*, Caleb said, were designed to let you into the world of the Kings. 'I think we're more comfortable as people and as a band. More comfortable to go with whatever sound or emotion we want. That's what this record was about to us – these emotions. Things we were feeling when we were on the road and away from home. We were having the great moments and the not-so-great moments, and that's what this record is about. It's not about a style, or trying to bump you up, or make you cry; I want there to be everything in-between.'

The bass line at the beginning of 'Razz' draws the listener into the track – and that's appropriate, since it was originally written about the bassist himself. 'Jared is "The Razzle Kid",' Caleb told the *NME*. 'I don't know what it was he did that day to piss me off so much I had to go write a song about it, because he pretty much pisses me off all the time. Everyone in this band is always pissing each other off.' He also added 'I wrote the song about him because it had the coolest bass line on the album. He loves playing it!'

Jared could lay aside his bass for most of the next track, as the Kings stripped it down and laid it bare for the acoustic folk number 'Day Old Blues'. It was a large departure from previous work; the closest thing previously performed by the band was 'Dusty' but that song lacked the maturity and cynical observation of lines like 'Girls are gonna love the way I toss my hair/boys are gonna hate the way I seem.'

It had been a quick but emotional process penning the track, Caleb revealed: 'The rest of the guys had decided to go shopping, and I was sitting on the hotel balcony with my guitar. I was thinking about my Mom a lot, and I just started playing and singing. When they got back I was crying. I've never cried while writing a song, and I've never written a song that quickly.'

Caleb put the broadening of musical style across the whole album down to the band having confidence in their own ability. But there was more. 'We've just changed as musicians, we're all a lot better at what we do. We can challenge ourselves to do things that are harder, things that we might have wanted to do on the first album but we weren't good enough.'

As if to highlight the stark contrast between musical

sounds and styles, the stomping classic 'Four Kicks'
followed immediately after. It was the second single to be
released from *Aha Shake Heartbreak*, reaching Number
24 in January 2005. The video stuck to the requirement
of a Kings of Leon performance with an added twist. 'We
really hate to do videos that aren't performance if they're
going to include us,' Caleb revealed. 'So it's a performance
video, but it's a big catastrophe; there are a lot of things
going on around us, and a lot of illusions; things you're
seeing but you really aren't. A lot of trick photography
that's really mind-blowing.'

The video incorporated all of this in the form of the
Kings playing in a waiting room full of people. A red mist
descends on them when the band start playing, resulting
in a mass brawl breaking out. With freeze-frames during
Caleb's vocals, Kings of Leon were heading for big
production. The video certainly matched the mood of the
track with its lyrics about rival gangs – frantic and angry,
with violent guitar riffs.

The penultimate track 'Velvet Snow' was another
120-second burst of 100 mile an hour rock'n'roll.
Nathan's rolling drums power the track through to a
thrashing chorus as Jared glues the verse together with
his pacing bass. The stop-start end to the record finished
with 'Remero', a measured track dominated by Jared's
simple bass beat, swinging to and fro. It was to become
the traditional way the Kings bowed out on their albums,
leaving the listener content rather than gasping for air.

The media reacted favourably Kings of Leon's 'second
debut', though some claimed there was a piece of the
puzzle still missing. *Rolling Stone* restrained themselves
from hurling out the superlatives, instead describing the
band to their largely unsuspecting American audience as

'a great young rock'n'roll band from Tennessee that has made two nearly great albums. *Aha Shake Heartbreak* is the second one, and like the first, 2003's *Youth And Young Manhood*… is just a handful of kicks and shivers short of pulverising excellence.'

However, the magazine favoured the purity of the album's production over 'the desperate airplay measures that marred many later Ramones albums,' but suggested 'it may be time for the Kings to take a chance with someone who knows how to build the kind of ambience that comes down like a hammer.'

New Musical Express naturally championed the record, gushing 'Clearly, somehow, somewhere on the never-ending tour that followed the release of *Youth And Young Manhood*, the Kings lost several key parts of their minds, in particular the ones that make bands release the same old shit, drawn from the same drained, dry old well, year in year out.'

The BBC also praised the album, stating that 'Musically it is innovative and diverse and Caleb's vocal style is as individual as ever. His rasping chords sounds like he's just smoked 50 fags but he remains tuneful and purveys strong emotion – whether exhilaration, tenderness or pain.'

The Guardian went into school report mode, describing the album as 'neither a weak facsimile of *Youth And Young Manhood* nor an alienating attempt to completely rebuild their sound. It just sounds like a vast improvement: the songwriting more adventurous, the palette of inspiration wider.' Top marks, then, though the reviewer claimed the band 'must try harder' with writing the lyrics, which he said 'come in two varieties: garbage and pretentious garbage…. It is less malevolent than witless – the kind of thing you would expect from a bunch of rednecks that have suddenly found themselves rock stars, with all the attendant trappings.'

Caleb's lyrics proved to be the main bone of contention with reviewers, many branding them 'obtuse' and overtly 'misogynistic', with the influential US *Pitchfork Media* website slamming Caleb's voice: 'He is a terrible singer, like a drunken Randy Newman with Tourette's – which would be a compliment if it didn't make you expect more intelligent lyrics…. He's shooting for some sort of Southern-slash-Appalachian accent, but ultimately he defies geography and just sounds unnatural.' Harsh words indeed, but the reviewer then backtracks somewhat crediting the band with having 'improved tenfold. They're tighter, more dynamic, and much more confident on *Aha Shake Heartbreak* than they were on *Youth And Young Manhood.*'

Caleb, for his part, held his hands up to the 'obtuse' nature of some of his lyrics, and even the incoherent way he delivered them. 'I never really expect people to understand what I'm saying. I know the way I phrase certain things, people aren't necessarily going to get it. We included the lyrics to *Aha Shake Heartbreak* in the CD, because on the last record people would try to guess what we were saying and they'd make us sound like idiots.' There was now an extra incentive for the fan to look inside the lyrics to find the meaning.

One thing all the critics seemed to agree on, be they positive or negative, was that the band never seemed to be more than a few sentences away from a comparison with another band or genre. Despite favouring the album, the reviewer on the *Allmusic* website was seemingly unable to describe the band without placing them in a frame of reference: 'Their success in the UK is understandable, as Caleb Followill's lazy drawl sounds like a cross between

(AC/DC's) Bon Scott, (the Kinks') Ray Davies and Eddie Money with a slight Jamaican accent, but it's their seamless and agreeable blend of rock'n'roll, country, and (13th Floor Elevators') Roky Erikson-style psychedelia, matched with a keen lyrical wit, that makes them fascinating to both sides of the pond.'

While realising the inevitability of comparisons in the media, the Kings were loathe to accept them, Jared telling *MusicOMH*: 'Every new band that comes out they label the new Killers or Strokes. But it's really hard – styles can pigeonhole you and we're constantly changing.' Caleb agreed. 'It's never been important to try and name what it is we do. I don't know what we do."

Despite the album garnering mostly positive reviews, many questioned the longevity of the band. The UK alternative radio station XFM stated: 'The parallels with the Strokes are greater than ever – a second album which suffers the dual distractions of high expectation and intense personal upheaval. But the band provide enough peaks to mostly keep on course. Whether they'll survive for another one is anyone's guess.' Many agreed that the Kings needed to take their music to the next level on their third album.

In the immediate aftermath of the album's release, the band embarked on a spate of UK dates – extended several times due to overwhelming demand – taking in cult rock venues from London's Brixton Academy to Nottingham's Rock City. The dates were placed in jeopardy through Nathan suffering from a kidney infection, but he survived. 'The minute he walked on stage, he felt a lot better,' Caleb told *NME* after the opening date in Manchester. 'The adrenaline of the show got him through it. Our guitar tech has been on stand-by in case Nathan's too ill to finish the tour. Hopefully Nathan will be well enough to finish these British dates.'

The eldest Followill completed the tour, which meant a lot to the band. Caleb revealed that they thought their performance at Glastonbury in the summer had been below par. 'It's unbelievable. The British crowds are so humbling. They sing back every word so it doesn't matter if I get the words wrong! The crowds are so happy to be here. We feel we had a bit to prove because we didn't do Glastonbury much justice when we played there this year.'

Matthew also lauded the UK crowds and was happy for the band to be touring in their own right. 'The last time we were here it was festivals and stuff, and that's fun, but it's a lot better when it's your own show – you get to hang out with your own fans after and stuff like that.'

With the album released in the UK and its US release to follow shortly, the Kings announced yet more tour dates – this time in America. Their jaunt would coincide with the release of *Aha Shake Heartbreak*, and the band would travel around the West Coast. Caleb was excited about playing their fellow countrymen new material and showing them what they had been missing. 'It's a lot like the first time we came [to the UK] because now the people know about us and we're starting in smaller venues and working our way up, but the crowd are like the UK crowd were at first – they want it so bad. We're looking to put some time into America and hopefully it's going to continue to grow.'

But it would be a support slot for a group of Irish rock giants that would garner the most interest. After meeting on Saturday-morning UK TV music show *CD:UK*, Kings of Leon were offered to open for U2 on the US leg of their Vertigo World Tour. The band would swap 500-capacity ballrooms for venues topping 20,000 fans – it would be something they would have to get used to. Jared said of the union: 'We got to go backstage and meet the guys and they were really down to earth and really awesome. We talked to them for a long while and they said something like "If we keep making great records that they would open up for *us*" and we all laughed, and I puked up in my mouth a little bit as I was so nervous!'

Nathan told MTV that their relative lack of awareness of the U2 phenomenon had helped the rest of the band curb their nervousness about the gigs. 'Growing up, we weren't allowed to listen to U2, so an album like *The Joshua Tree* [released in 1987], we just discovered that like two years ago. If we were a band that had grown up listening to U2, we'd be a hell of a lot more scared than we are. But what we do take from U2 is the realisation of how great it would be to be a band for 20 years. We can only fathom how great we could potentially become as long as we keep our heads on straight and don't get married and divorced two or three times.'

For proof of how the Kings grew up on the U2 jaunt, we have only to consult the *Nashville Scene* website review of a pre-tour show they played at the Exit/In club in their hometown that February. They say prophets are without honour in their own country, but local scribes Elizabeth Orr and Marie Yarbrough took the Kings to task with such sharpened claws it was tempting to believe they might just have been spurned former girlfriends.

'If there was anything beyond bland Southern rock going on here,' spat Marie, 'I couldn't hear it. Caleb Followill, the lead singer, looked like he was totally bored, just spitting out meaningless words.'

Her partner weighed in on the Kings' fashion statement: 'The cut-up draped-neck T-shirt the guitarist was wearing

was the most repulsive fashion statement I've ever seen. If
these boys are renowned for their hip style, I'm frightened.
Their hair resembled structured layered mullets, though
Caleb Followill went for swift undercurls that refused to
frizz. Actually, I think that's the reason he remained stiff
throughout the show: he was afraid he'd mess up his hair.
And the bassist's earring, glistening in the lights during his
profile poses, Jeez! The entire band was groomed... like
they were playing a garage band in a movie.'

'I still don't get why people love their music,' said
Marie. 'The Southern rock thing has been done and
done better. I was expecting at least some glimmer of
personality.' 'And no matter how mind-blowing they
could have been,' Elizabeth opined, 'nothing would have
excused the lead singer casually pulling out his cell phone
onstage. What was he doing? Checking the time? Seeing
if he had any messages? Did he think he'd make a call or
two?' Perhaps Caleb was making a call to Bono saying
'Get me out of here....'

In any event, and despite this critical mauling, Kings of
Leon played a mammoth 28 dates with the Irish legends,
taking in arenas from Anaheim's Arrowhead Pond to
Madison Square Garden from March to May 2005, and
were the longest-serving support act on the entire tour.
Jared reflected on the experience, claiming the band felt
the pressure of the expansive arenas: 'Nobody pressured
us except for ourselves. Just getting up there in front of 10
or 12,000 people and it only being half-full, but it was still
a shitload of people. And we just had to learn how to not
give them one second to be able to say something. It was
like 45 minutes of music and so we barely had a chance
to listen to them cheer because we'd just keep playing.
Because we didn't want fucking hecklers or anything like

that. By the end I think we won over a lot of the crowds.'

The Kings had no need to worry about acceptance when they returned to their most fervent fans in the summer on yet another tour of the UK. Jared explained that, despite the warmth shown by the British faithful, the band weren't particularly skilled in conversing with the audience, though it was something he believed would come in time. 'We still haven't become one hundred per cent comfortable playing in front of people; we'll be playing the songs and in between we'll be talking about it – who messed up and who did whatever – and so we forget to even say anything to the crowd.'

What they lacked in crowd interaction they more than made up for in showmanship and all-round foundation-shaking rock. One review from a date in Brighton remarked: 'The Followill clan appeared aloof and nonchalant as ever as they strolled on stage, but thankfully as soon as they picked up their instruments, it was clear that this was going to be a roller-coaster ride to remember.... For their 20-song set, they played like stadium-rock veterans, like they *belonged* in venues like this.'

New Musical Express commented after a gig at London's Hammersmith Apollo that the evolution of the band's recorded music was now also reflected in their live shows. 'There's a more focused intensity about the Followills these days. Oldies "Molly's Chambers" and "Wasted Time" – occasionally muddy and flat live – have been fed on a strict steroid diet and sound utterly enormous. However, it's the newer material, taken from *Aha Shake Heartbreak* that's most impressive. "Slow Night, So Long" is a sleazy blast of pure guitar belligerence, while "Four Kicks" sees pints launched skywards and the Apollo struggle to contain the explosions of delirium from the assembled throng.'

Touring long into the summer and beyond – including warming up the crowds for the Foo Fighters at the Reading and Leeds Festivals – Kings of Leon were cementing their reputation not only as a great live band but a hard-working one too. It was undeniable they had successfully negotiated the dreaded sophomore album. They were rapidly coming to the attention of an even wider audience than had assembled after *Youth And Young Manhood*, thanks to a more mature and polished sound. But the balance between critical and commercial success is a delicate one and, though becoming more popular, it was generally agreed among critics that to reach the next level the band needed to evolve their sound, image and lyrical content.

Caleb was one step ahead of them. 'I think we touched on something the other day that no band has really touched on, which immediately gave me chill bumps, and I think I saw a vision of where Kings of Leon are going next. If we can do it, we're gonna skip ahead a few generations.' Far from being a band that basked in the glory of what had already been achieved, they were already planning what to do next. After all, they had many years of musical inspiration and growth to catch up on – the Kings were hoping their next move would mean checkmate in the success game.

CHAPTER FIVE

CHANGING TIMES

Musically speaking, the experiences of 2005 had stood the Kings of Leon in good stead. Not least the first leg of U2's Vertigo Tour, two months which saw them travel from San Diego to Boston via New York and Los Angeles. It was an experience that would leave a noticeable mark on their next recording, especially in the guitar department.

Caleb explained the process. 'If you hear a band and say, "Yeah, we want to go on the road with them" then obviously it's because you're a fan of theirs. And if they say "yes", it's because they're a fan of yours. Then you're kind of living with each other for a little while – you give your take on what you think they sound like.'

Jared took up the story: 'We've just become friends with a lot of bands and once you become friends with a band you kind of take on their style of music – bands grow together. A lot of the people that we tour with we end up sounding like. And when we see them next, they'll tell us that they feel like they're ripping us off.'

The Edge had been impressed by the way the Kings 'are taking a Southern American idiom and moving it into the twenty-first century. We saw it on the tour: they were learning so much. They were so hungry to see what was going on.' Nathan thought it 'a huge deal, getting offered to go open for the biggest band in the world, especially since we didn't even know that they knew us, much less knew our music.'

Yet there'd been a notable press backlash against the Kings, and that was inevitable given the big push they'd been given by *New Musical Express* as the band to watch. Once upon a time Britain had four music papers that came out weekly, but only the *NME* now survived. This gave what they said extra weight, but it also meant that the recipient of their largesse could feel a backlash from all quarters once – or even before – their 15 minutes had expired. And with internet sites and blogs now filling the gap left by the demise of *Sounds, Melody Maker* and *Record Mirror,* there were plenty of soapboxes from which anti-Kings sentiment was being spouted.

The new recipients of the *NME* seal of approval were the Arctic Monkeys, a Sheffield outfit. 'We won't play *Top Of The Pops*', announced frontman Alex Turner, in an attempt to mimic the Clash – but the band's clever use of the Internet meant there was a huge demand for their music, even before they had officially released anything. They gave their blessing to fans copying and distributing their music, and their following mushroomed as tracks were swapped in a classic example of viral marketing on the Internet. According to one estimate there were already 142 different versions of various Arctic Monkeys songs floating around on the Internet by the time of their first official release.

By January 2006, the Arctic Monkeys were the most searched-for band on the Internet, their website the most visited in the Bands and Artists category. The Followills had followed a much older template in slogging the outposts of rock'n'roll, paying their dues in time-honoured fashion, rather than travelling the information superhighway. And that, in some eyes, made them old hat.

'The Arctic Monkeys were everywhere,' Caleb would later reflect ruefully. 'We used to read magazines and people would always refer to us. When it stops you get jealous. We're so competitive that when we hear a good record by someone we think "all right, if that's what we gotta beat we're gonna do our best."'

What was worse was that the constant touring and abuse of drugs and alcohol had seen Kings of Leon returning to their Nashville base in a state of disarray, the members cordially disliking each other. Blood might have been thicker than water, but in this instance they'd reached a turning point. 'We went from being best friends to being enemies,' Caleb admitted, while Jared blamed 'communication problems…the only way to understand and fix things is by getting into an argument.'

But there was never any question of such petty disagreements derailing the gravy train. And, as the eventful year of 2005 drew to a close, Jared told *New Musical Express* that Kings of Leon were already planning their next album. 'We've written a shitload right now. We're writing so much every day. We've probably got at least seven or eight songs. We're really confident and I feel like we write the best song every fucking day. This is kind of the beginning of what Kings of Leon are to be.'

Jared had predicted 'We may go into the studio in November,' but the boys sensibly gave themselves Christmas off to rest up and recuperate, never mind lick the occasional wound. It was in fact early 2006 that the band set about the task of creating what would become their first long-playing chart-topper in the United Kingdom.

The maxim 'Don't mend what ain't broken' now came into play as the group stuck with long-time musical partner Angelo Petraglia and second-generation producer Ethan Johns to oversee proceedings. This was entirely understandable after the success of *Aha Shake Heartbreak*, though Nathan admitted they did entertain the idea of a clean break. 'We met with other producers. We told them the kind of record we wanted to make and kinda got their feedback, but at the end of the day it just made more sense....'

Caleb added: 'There's a lot of misconception in what people think of our writing relationship – it's not what they think. In the beginning, at the beginning only, before I was confident, [Angelo] was pretty much a guy to bounce ideas off – a mentor. Now he's pretty much a producer and we still bounce ideas off him in the studio. Ethan Jones is behind the boards and Angelo's there with two middle fingers up saying, "Come on, motherfuckers, pump me up!"'

Even though the recording was completed in a matter of weeks, the boys' third album would take a year to come together, from first entering the studio to its eventual release. The reason behind the delay was the cramped release schedule of their record label. With such an important record, the band didn't want to get marginalised by parent company Sony BMG focusing on – at that point, at least – their more lucrative artists. (RCA, owned by the European BMG – Bertelsmann Music Group – had merged with the larger Sony concern in 2004, as the music business went through a turbulent period.)

'It's all about the quarters with our label,' a business-savvy Nathan explained. 'First quarter, second quarter, third quarter, fourth quarter and the last thing we wanted to do was be competing with (superstars) Beyonce and Justin Timberlake. We're like "fuck it, we'll compete with (middle of the road artists) Yanni and Kenny G when they come out in the second quarter and we will kick their *ass*".'

As for the recording venue, the band stayed closer to their roots, switching between their tried and trusted base in Nashville at the Blackbird Studios and Sunset Sound in Los Angeles – the former being a second home for country giants Sheryl Crow and Tim McGraw. An earthy, rootsy undercurrent would indeed be prevalent on the album, but this time the Kings were aiming big – arena big. Jared told *NME* 'We all feel like; "Man, this record is going to be so big! Not big as in record sales, but just in the way it sounds and how much better... it's going to be a lot more anthemic than anything we've done."'

Caleb echoed his brother's sentiments and issued a rallying cry. 'We're sick of being considered an indie band that opens for other bands. We feel we have something to show and something to prove, and just want to throw it all out there.' The album, while different to the Kings' first two, would not be a total departure, more a development of the family's style and experiences.

Making the album in Nashville had a positive effect on the quartet, home comforts proving beneficial to the recording process. As Matthew said after the album's release: 'This time we had the comfort of sleeping in our own beds. And it was cool because you could drive to the studio in your own car and listen to the songs you just did, giving you the chance to figure out whether you wanted to add or change anything to the song. It was definitely a big thing to this record of just feeling comfortable and being able to do whatever we wanted to do with the songs.' Also, the Kings had long ago lost their recording virginity and, while by no means old hands, were more comfortable with their instruments and no longer backwards in coming forward with suggestions to improve the end result.

The Blackbird Studios themselves were also a positive source of inspiration to the band. John McBride's venue could be altered to suit the mood of each song as the boys laid down the tracks. 'It was the best studio, man – you could change the colour of the room to whatever you wanted,' Caleb enthused. 'Say with a song like "Arizona", we'd make it pink and purple in there, or with a song like "Charmer", we'd make it a harsh red. We got to play around with stuff like that and that made the vibe come out so much.'

The Kings had taken a back seat to Petraglia and Johns in previous albums, but this time around they wanted to have a more prominent role in the recording and production processes. As previously suggested, their familiarity with proceedings had emboldened them to become more involved, a natural progression from the diffident days of old.

As Nathan explained, this album was going to show the true Kings of Leon: the band they had evolved into, rather than the four enthusiastic neophytes who had cut their first record. 'We wanted to go for the sounds that we were hearing in our heads, because your record represents you as a band. But when you're young, as we were when we made our first two albums, we didn't know that.'

During the recording period, the Kings were also

out and about on the concert circuit, rubbing shoulders with those at the musical summit. After playing nearly 30 dates with U2 on the previously mentioned US leg of their 'Vertigo' tour in 2005, they were requested to open for rock legend Bob Dylan on nine dates of his 'Modern Times' tour of America – by the man himself! An indication of how this boosted their profile and status can be gauged by the fact that the support slots on other legs of the tour were filled by two more established acts, Foo Fighters and Jack White's Raconteurs. It was an indication of how they were already making waves in influential circles.

Indeed, Dylan was on something of a roll in commercial terms. *Modern Times* had become the veteran singer-songwriter's first Number 1 album in the US since 1976's *Desire*. It was also his first album to debut at the summit of the *Billboard* chart, selling an impressive 191,933 copies in its first week. At the tender age of 65, Dylan became the oldest living person to have an album enter the US charts at Number 1.

He was, of course, one of the Kings' acknowledged early influences, and they were understandably surprised that he was a fan. This fact would become clear after one date they played together. 'We thought that someone in his camp had asked us to open for him,' Caleb told *Rolling Stone* magazine, 'but he let us know it was actually him. He asked me, "What's that last song you played in the set?" I said "Trani". He said, "That's a hell of a song." Later, when I was in bed, I thought, "Did he *really* say that?"'

A handful of Australian tour dates with grunge gods Pearl Jam also fuelled the group's desire to break out and create something special with their third album. Matthew admitted touring with such a high-flying band inspired the sound for the upcoming album. 'There were a lot of big, open rooms with a lot of reverb and we liked the way that it sounded. So we thought that the next record we made needed to sound like we're playing in a large arena with a huge sound.' Pearl Jam mainman Eddie Vedder would later return the compliment by taking a copy of *Aha Shake Heartbreak*, the album they'd been promoting, with him for inspiration to a remote island while writing new songs.

Ethan Johns echoed this, noting the venues the Kings opened in proved a major inspiration for the direction of the new album. 'The biggest thing that's influenced the material on this album,' he told *Mix* magazine 'is the fact that they'd been writing a lot of it during soundchecks in arenas — big sound, the tempos are slower, things thematically are bigger.' The Kings no longer wanted to play the dingy clubs and ballrooms; they were destined for better things.

Despite such burgeoning ambition, the album's recording process was typically laid-back, the way the brothers like to lay down tracks. But record-label rep Steve Ralbovsky made it clear that everyone involved was taking it seriously, particularly after mixing with Dylan, U2 and other megastars. 'It's that challenging third album, and musically they've taken it further than anybody thought they were capable of five years ago. Some of it stems from the musical inspiration of the people they've been around lately, some of it's their own instincts and they've gotten much more confidence and prowess as musicians, so they're not afraid to stretch out a bit.'

In September 2006 the band announced the name of their forthcoming release. Another homage to their pentecostal roots, the album was named *Because Of The Times*, after one of the many religious conferences the boys attended during their youth, the three-day event a highlight in the brothers' young lives. 'You'd pick your favourite preachers like you'd pick your favourite bands,' Nathan told *The Independent*. Yet despite the title's Christian connotations, the album's subject-matter would be far from saintly.

Because Of The Times would take a much slower and calculating tone than the plucky Southern rock sound of *Aha Shake Heartbreak*. The Kings were maturing, and their newest material would reflect this. One critic described it as 'a dark, noisy journey into the dick-swinging male ego, with songs about fucking, fighting and leaving before dawn'.

Caleb agreed, at least up to a point. 'It's more about ideas, man,' he reasoned. 'We're not singing about our dick anymore, we're singing about the *consequences* of our dick.' The frenetic folk guitars of 'King Of The Rodeo' would be replaced by the pacey strumming and distorted vocals of 'My Party', while the made-for-radio hit sound of 'The Bucket' would be exchanged for the laid-back but equally accessable anthem of 'Fans'. As *New Musical Express*, their perennial champions, put it, 'a little growing up goes a long way'.

Even the album's front cover went black, in stark contrast to their previous two efforts. It was this darker side that would be evident in 'On Call', the first single released in the lead-up to the album's release. 'It's got [a] great little bass part,' Ethan Johns said of the track during recording. 'It's relatively easy to swallow, but it's still got bags of attitude.' The same could be said of the album as a whole.

'The record definitely had more of an arena influence to it,' Nathan would later reflect. 'The songs were bigger, more airy... we could imagine the songs played in these big places.' Matthew's guitar tone in particular now had more than a hint of a certain Irish six-stringer to it. As one reviewer put it 'If you really want to time-line the ascension of the Kings, track the guitar work of cousin Matthew Followill, who's gone from restless, backwoods noodler to someone looking to replace The Edge. You can pinpoint KoL's transition from cult fave to major star in the song "On Call". Matthew's licks are suddenly hopeful, epic, feel-good. Not dangerous, but dazzling.'

It was indeed 'On Call' that would set the tone for an edgier style that would be apparent throughout their new album. 'When you fall to pieces, Lord, you know I'll be there laughing,' sang Caleb, giving notice that this album was not to be about high-school romances or romantic folly. Fans embraced this new direction, as 'On Call' charted at Number 18 in March 2007, a full 23 places up on 'King Of The Rodeo' two years previously.

The video matched the dark overtones of the song, the intro seeing the band dressed in black, bathed in a white background. There is a flash of stage lights, and the backdrop changes to an eerie forest. The simplicity of the shoot allowed the camera to focus on Caleb's facial expressions to convey the song's emotion.

The album's first track, 'Knocked Up', stretched over a seven-minute period – in stark contrast to their previous short and explosive tracks that Caleb had threatened were designed to 'punch you in the balls'. The song charted a teenager's journey from anxieties over his impending fatherhood to a determination to be a parent. Unusually, it appeared to have four verses but no chorus – indeed, the title appeared nowhere in the lyrics at all.

Caleb said of the inspiration behind the track: 'We've been accused of things and we've had people say that we have children and it's just bullshit. But it kinda makes you think. As I was admiring the things I had, I also realised I kind of didn't have anyone to share it with. And I questioned if I was man enough to stand up for a challenge like that if it were to come along.'

It was perhaps a strange subject for the band to tackle at this point, but the thoughtful and epic opener set the rest of the album apart as a clear departure from all that had gone before. And the listener only had to go as far as track two, the frenzied 'Charmer', to have this confirmed.

This frenetic track, with Caleb's primal wailing and Jared's bass guitar thumping in the background, came in just short of three minutes and was the perfect antidote to the measured opener. 'A howling, primal, downright unsettling but ultimately rewarding listen', said one impressed reviewer.

The track's accompanying video was another simple shoot, with the band playing to an empty theatre, perhaps a nod to performing to half-full venues while on tour with U2. The video again focused on Caleb's delivery of the song, his frenzied actions and expressions something never before seen in a Kings video.

There was a new spirit of adventure aboard, and, as Jared told *Mix* magazine, his instrument was at the heart of it. 'On a lot of records, you can't hear the bass at all, and the bass on this record is different. 'One song, I was like, "I just need a little bit more bass," and you could tell that Ethan was pissed, and he told the assistant, "All right, turn it up 1.5 decibels" to teach us a lesson, cos it was obviously gonna be way too loud. And he did it, and everybody listened to it, and everybody was like, "Yep, it's great — that's it," and we kept it there.'

It was apparent that this was a band buoyed up with

confidence in the studio, hitting full maturity as performers and, most importantly, songwriters. As Nathan told *New Musical Express*, 'We weren't scared to try anything. Every song showed us something we had inside of ourselves that we didn't know existed, which enabled us to be even bolder on the next song.'

And bolder they became. After 'On Call', with its menacing bass line and bittersweet feel, came 'McFearless' – centred once again around Jared's bass, this time distorting it for the opening of the track. It shared centre stage alongside Caleb's throaty delivery of the chorus, a primal scream of 'It's my show/I must go/With my soul'. While the Kings could never be accused of lacking soul, on the evidence so far it was being laid bare in a fashion unseen in the previous two albums.

The band wanted to move away from being pigeonholed as a made-for-radio Southern rock cliché, the favourite claim of their detractors. 'We wanted to challenge ourselves,' Nathan said, 'and we wanted to fuck with people's heads in the sense of, you're not gonna get a record full of two-and-a-half minute barn-burners that are undeniably Kings of Leon. We wanted to not only challenge ourselves, but challenge our fans. Obviously you wanna grow with each record and you wanna make it a little better than the ones before.'

In contrast, 'Black Thumbnail' began with the jaunty Southern feel of past efforts, and ploughed head-on to a heavy, riff-laden chorus that was typical of the new era of Kings of Leon. Plucked guitars and distorted vocals continued through 'My Party' while 'True Love Way' slowed things down for the first time since 'Knocked Up'. Even so, the song still retained that stadium quality the boys said they were looking for.

Kings of Leon: Caleb, Jared, Matthew and
Nathan Followill. Spain, November 2004.

Nathan gives the toms some serious stick. Kings of Leon US tour, May 2007.

Caleb, performing at T In The Park 2009, 10 July, Kinross, Scotland. The very last performance with this particular Gibson....

Headlining at Glastonbury, Friday 27 June, 2008.
'An absolute milestone... we felt we'd really made it....'

US tour May 2007. Left to right: Caleb, Jared, Matthew

Not the American South – but Doncaster, England, May 2007.
The UK had almost become the band's adopted home...

The story of brothers who escaped from a strict religious background...? Nathan and Caleb, Glastonbury, 2007.

The band skipped through the verses of 'Ragoo', singing 'Here's to the kids out there smoking in the streets/They're way too young/ but I'm way too old to preach'. Still only in his mid-twenties, Caleb admitted 'I know I'm young. But I'm an old soul'. *Because Of The Times* may have reflected a more mature sound and lyrical content, yet the carnal and hedonistic core of the Kings was still alive and kicking.

The album headed into its final stretch with the heartfelt anthem 'Fans', on which the Kings sing in an almost down-home, acoustic style about the perks of being sat on the pedestals of fame. Given their continued low profile in their native United States, this was widely interpreted as homage to their British fan base, and sure enough the tribute landed them at Number 13 in the UK chart – their highest-ranking single to date. Yet their homeland was – disappointingly – still less enthusiastic for the Tennessee natives, as the track still failed to register in any of the US charts.

'The Runner' slowed things right down, the opening verse stripped back to just Nathan on drums and a single bass line as Caleb, in typically confident form, claimed 'I talk to Jesus/Jesus says I'm OK'. It was a song Caleb had written 'when I was pretty down and partying hard', and was known to his friends as 'the Jesus song'.

The guitars then kick in and the track builds up to a crescendo, but never quite reaches it. The mood then returns to an eerie calm, as the album slips almost unnoticeably into 'Trunk'. This again is measured and slow, focusing on the double punch of percussion and Caleb's strong vocals. Reviewers at *NME* said, 'As ever with Kings of Leon, this record is a song or two too long', possibly pointing the finger at 'Trunk' as they did so, but it could be seen as the Kings 'warming down' after the frantic highs of 'McFearless' and 'My Party'.

The album closed with two varying tracks: 'Camaro' and 'Arizona'. The former picked the pace back up with some catchy guitar hooks and solos that were notably absent from the previous two songs, while the final track of *Because Of The Times* combined a feeling of reflection with a massive arena sound. 'Arizona' was an epic that had clear echoes of classic U2 circa their 'Joshua Tree' eighties heyday. Yet no-one could say that it was in any way pompous.

The song offered a poignant ending to the album, as Caleb muses 'I kinda think I like her/I kinda think I do...', perhaps an indication that the Kings were at long last reconsidering their vagrant ways. *New Musical Express* concurred, summarising that this was 'an album all about growing up and moving on.' They also pointed out that, by the 2 April release date, Jared was almost old enough to buy his own drinks....

Indeed the lifestyle of debauchery indulged in by the group was beginning to be curtailed, in particular the well-publicised drugtaking. As if making up for lost youth, the Kings found themselves embracing a plethora of taboo substances once exposed to the real world outside of their heavily religious Southern bubble. This was beginning to have a negative effect on both the band's working and personal relationships. The fact that they were being worked hard by management and record company was scarcely helping, either.

'We were getting to the end of our rope,' Caleb told *Uncut*. 'On tour we were going at it so much that we had to rely on "things" just to keep going, we were always fighting. It took a while, but you slowly started to see people look better, and be nicer, and you realised it was because they weren't doing any drugs.' Not suprisingly he revealed the band – and family – were stronger as a result of their experiences. 'Only then did we all became friends again – having dinner and doing fun stuff together, playing golf and shit and just enjoying each other's company – both as part of the band and outside of it. Now it feels like we're all brothers again.'

Matthew agreed. 'I don't know, man. I think we caught up for all those lost years in our first couple years of the band. When we started out we had been so sheltered and stuff that we kind of went crazy for the first couple of years, and we kind of ripped our way through with a kind of rebellion so we could get that all out of our system. Now we're kind of pretty chilled, we don't really do anything but drink.' By no means a teen-pop quartet, Kings of Leon had nevertheless crammed a lifetime of experiences into less than a decade – and could offer them to the world through their songs.

With narcotics now in the past and a clearer set of heads to focus on the music, the amount of personal investment poured into the album by the Followills ensured that anticipation was rife with how the media and world at large would react to their latest offering. Jared said of the album 'I think for this whole thing we just started to realise, and we never really thought of it this way, but if this was to be our last record, I think we'd be cool with it – as far as what we've done. We've made a record that we're all perfectly satisfied with.' Much more than a tidy 40-minute package of instant hooks and radio friendly riffs, *Because Of The Times* was the boys' labour of love, and while acceptance wasn't mandatory, it was certainly welcome and, indeed, hoped for.

Because Of The Times was well reviewed - nowhere more so than in *Q* magazine, who made it one of their picks of 2007. They saw a mighty stylistic leap from the 'Southern Strokes' of the first two albums. The new effort, they proclaimed, was 'therefore a revelation, the work of a band who'd clearly taken notes on interim tour supports with Pearl Jam, Bob Dylan and, most audibly, U2.' It sparkled, they concluded, 'with a stadium-sized epic rock sheen.'

Nathan was delighted with the news. 'Awesome, man,' he exclaimed. 'We had no idea,' adding that he'd be buying his family magazine subscriptions for Christmas. Acknowledging that they were moving to target a more mature audience, he joked 'The next album we'll be going for senior citizens… and toddlers.' If that sent mixed messages, he was at least pleased that 'the way we were raised could've pigeonholed us – but thankfully people realised we made decent music.' More ruefully, he concluded with the admission that 'We're so busy we don't have time to go wild and crazy any more.'

New Musical Express, the Kings' traditional print-media supporters, praised the album, acknowledging the attempt at a more diverse and mature selection of music, despite perhaps sacrificing the amount of airtime the tracks might receive. 'Following on from the precedent set by *Aha Shake Heartbreak*, Kings of Leon are revealing themselves to be one of those bands whose records get progressively more fascinating as they get older, unconcerned that the lack of tunes could see their sales slump. Radical New Direction is a bit strong, but it's clear that KoL, along with long-time producer Ethan Johns, have been striving to add a new dimension to a band previously accused of having all the depth of a puddle.'

Going on to describe it as 'without doubt the best thing the band have ever recorded', the BBC music website also saluted the band's dedication to create a body of work, the songs working both individually and collectively, but at the risk of less commercial success. 'It's clever-with-a-kick attitude will quite possibly deny commercial success beyond mid-teen chart positions, (but) this new sound is simply too evolved for the 'first album' frenzy that renders [other bands] forgettably catchy.'

Any fears of commercial success being sacrificed in the pursuit of creativity were laid to rest when the album hit the UK Number 1 spot in April 2007, finally hitting gold (100,000 copies sold) after two bronze efforts. It also managed to climb to Number 25 in the US, offering real hope of a major breakthrough there and becoming their best-selling album on both sides of the Atlantic.

The new anthemic, arena-filling musical direction the band were aiming for was gradually bringing them further and further into the forefront of popular consciousness, and was a sign of things to come. Bigger songs meant bigger record sales, and it was a theme the band would happily continue.

Ethan Johns summed up the results of his and the band's labours. 'One of the most special things about them is their ability to allow a spiritual elevation to occur during a performance — getting something going and feeling it and creating that elation of spirit. That's what I'm going for in a take with them; it's when they hit that, that it all makes sense.'

Upon the album's release, the Sony BMG promotion machine went into well-oiled overdrive and the Kings soon found themselves embarking on 40 dates that would take them through the UK and onto America, showcasing the new material in the way it was intended – live.

There was only one problem – the tracks intended for venues such as Madison Square Garden and London's O2 Arena were initially restricted to London's Hammersmith Apollo and Chicago's Riviera Theatre. The former, though a respected venue, catered for just over 5,000, while the latter accommodates just over 2,000. The comparison is an indication of how the band still needed to break their home country, but neither was anywhere near the Kings' ultimate goal.

Still, fans packed out the venues to see the Kings power out the likes of 'Charmer' and 'My Party', before igniting the crowd with old favourites 'Trani' and 'The Bucket'. It was no frills rock'n'roll, giving the audience the songs they wanted in their rawest form, not hiding behind flashing lights and LCD screens. One reviewer said of the shows: 'Start to finish, they serve the rock up loud and fast. No jamming solos, no ironic covers, no transcendent or life-altering showstoppers: just hook-laden Southern-leaning rock with a sprinkling of indie sensibility. It is music capable of entertaining massive amounts of people at any given time.'

The band's effort to create a new live and large sound paid off when playing the new tracks, as Caleb explained. 'We don't ever wanna put a song on our record that we can't pull off live. We're a live band. At the end of the day that's what we're good at, that's what we do. On our worst day, we want our live show to at least equal the record. That's just par for the course.'

The 2007 summer festivals were an opportunity to play to ten times the number of fans, and served as a dress rehearsal for things to come. After gracing the South by Southwest music-business showcase in Austin, Texas, and Scotland's T in the Park Festival, the band arrived at the

2007 Carling Weekend at Reading and Leeds. Occupying the second headline spot to Razorlight, and with Caleb sporting a new cropped hairstyle and designer stubble, the Kings wooed the 80,000 fans and the band's reception was far more rapturous than the Anglo-Scandinavian quartet that followed. The Kings, by common consent, had blown Razorlight clean off the stage, and it was clear that future invitations to such events would require headline status to be offered and accepted. The Kings' volcano was close to a real eruption.

In June, midway through the tour, Nathan announced his engagement to girlfriend and musician Jessie Baylin, after he proposed to her in her family's restaurant in New York. Another connection made at Coachella Festival in California would have far-reaching implications for Caleb. For it was here that he met Lily Aldridge, the fashion model to whom he would later give the credit for straightening him out. Cocaine and whiskey were soon to be off limits… as far as the press was concerned, at least.

So while he had no woman problems to contend with, for the foreseeable future at least, Caleb had no intention of climbing 'on the wagon' any time soon. 'You drink for yourself,' he told *Mojo* magazine, adding 'you're so scared you'll wake up one day and you'll be absolutely normal because you don't have a vice.'

By the end of 2007, *Because Of The Times* had sold over 360,000 copies in the UK. When *Rolling Stone* magazine eulogised the album upon its release they mused, 'How good can the Kings of Leon get?' On *Because Of The Times*, they'd already gone further than anybody could have guessed or hoped. With the foundations for a fourth album already being laid, their public wouldn't have to wait long to find out.

CHAPTER SIX

SEX ON FIRE...

Fresh off touring *Because Of The Times*, Kings of Leon were basking in success, particularly in the United Kingdom. But something rankled with the band. Although they were playing larger venues in their home country than previously, the acceptance just wasn't present as it was on the other side of the ocean. Something had to change.

Caleb recounts how an appearance by British indie group the Arctic Monkeys – the band that used the Internet to gain a national following and who had usurped the Kings as *NME* darlings – on TV hit home with him and his bandmates. 'They were on (US TV prime-time showcase) *Saturday Night Live* and we've never been on there. I thought, "Man, we're from America and this bunch of kids from England come over here like the Beatles".' (As an aside, Matthew would go on to date Johanna Bennett, the former girlfriend of Arctic Monkeys singer Alex Turner.)

As each album progressed from its predecessor, moving from a gritty Southern folk-based sound to expansive stadium rock'n'roll, the Kings were getting closer and closer to US recognition, but Caleb for one felt it was long overdue. 'I'm sick of being big everywhere else,' he told *Rolling Stone* magazine. 'For America to kind of turn its back on us is heartbreaking.'

After the success of their third album, the band was a hot property in Europe. But as they brought their tour to a close in faraway New Zealand, the intention was to take a well-earned six months off to recharge the batteries and, crucially, get away from each other. As in previous years, they had been asked to appear at a number of festivals. These invitations had been politely declined, but when the Friday night headline slot at the 2008 Glastonbury Festival was dangled in front of their noses, a swift rethink was called for. After all, this had been the venue for their first ever festival appearance back in 2003. That had been followed by a second showing the next year. Now the opportunity had come up, it was tempting to return in triumph for a third time.

The invite was something of a last-minute affair, putting the Kings up there as headline attractions along with the re-formed Verve and controversially booked rapper Jay-Z. Holiday plans were rapidly put on hold and, with all leave cancelled, the Kings booked rehearsal space and resumed normal service. This was particularly tough on Caleb, whose scheduled surgery on his shoulder was swiftly brought forward.

'We were gonna take some time off,' Jared said of the decision, 'and we kind of found out that some of our dream shows became available to us… We were gonna headline Glastonbury and stuff like that so we kinda had to get on the ball quicker than we'd expected.' The honour, he felt, was well earned. 'A lot of people headline Glastonbury who don't deserve it. We deserve it as much some of the bands who've done it before.' When pressed, he admitted that he was thinking of the Arctic Monkeys and the Killers, both bands they'd 'put in more time than'.

The Kings' headline status was revealed on Radio 1's *Newsbeat* and came one week after the registration process for the festival was launched. The BBC reported that 'Kings of Leon may seem like a surprise choice for headliners, but they are an increasingly popular band and their selection is probably in keeping with Michael Eavis's attempt to appeal to younger music fans.' Speaking to *Newsbeat*, co-organiser Emily Eavis added that Kings of Leon were deserving of the top slot, having 'come through the ranks' at previous festivals. She felt they were ready to make the leap and would follow 'the great heritage of [past] Friday night headliners Coldplay and the White Stripes.'

But having been fixtures on the festival circuit for a couple of years, the Kings were aware they might be expected to have something to offer which the crowds hadn't heard before. Caleb added: 'We had a lot of festivals and big concerts and things calling to [the point] where we knew that, if we were gonna go back and play these places, we would wanna have some new songs and some new material to play'.

Many bands would have contented themselves with churning out a selection of B-sides or bonus tracks to fill the gap, but there was nothing half-hearted about the Kings' commitment. The demand for their services and the desire to gain acceptance in their home country put Kings of Leon back in the studio to create their fourth album, and their second in just 18 months. It was a case of riding the wave of popularity that had quickly amassed and rolled all the way across the North Atlantic. 'Because of the thrill of being Number One,' said Caleb, 'I think the songs we're writing now just really have something about them. It's a passion that I think will carry on. We try to strike while the iron's hot, and we're writing some really good songs right now.'

The album that resulted, the band's fourth, was to be seen as the next step in evolution for the Followills, whose sound and style on *Because Of The Times* had differed so vastly from the recklessly melodic firecrackers on their first two albums. Naturally, the boys stuck with Angelo Petraglia, and also bought in Grammy award winner Jacquire King, a sound engineer on *Aha Shake Heartbreak*. But long-time production presence Ethan Johns was a notable absentee.

Upon joining the team, King told *The Aquarian:* 'The growth you are seeing is the band wanting an opportunity to experiment on this record. They are becoming sonically adventurous and I think their best work is still in them. Based on their track record for the past four albums I feel they are in a position to take a big step after this record. I have seen them grow, and I can tell you the new album is tremendous. They just keep finding new things within themselves. All of that rings true. Kings of Leon have greater records to make.'

This was an opinion shared by the band. 'We knew this record was definitely gonna be our bold attempt at trying to make a record that wasn't necessarily obviously Kings of Leon' is how Nathan explained the decision to opt for King over Ethan Johns. 'And with the first two records with Ethan, as soon as you heard the first note of any song, you could tell it was definitely a Kings of Leon song, just based on the sound that Ethan got. So, going into this record, we knew that we wanted to step away from that sound.'

King was a producer with a passion for percussion – Caleb revealed he'd regularly take two hours of studio time tuning the kit while the rest of the band got steadily drunker – and it was Nathan's contribution on which the most time and effort was spent during the album sessions to ensure that there was more variation in the beats for the songs across the album. All his time spent in the gym was about to pay off handsomely.

Much store had been set within the band on third album *Because Of The Times* being their breakthrough album in the US, but the fact that it had gone so far and no further left them a target to aim at. 'We thought that record would take us to the next phase,' Nathan told *Mojo* magazine, 'but the fact that it didn't actually helped us out, cos when it came time to make (the next one) we thought, well, shit, if the last one didn't do it, then fuck it, we don't need to worry if this is the one's gonna do it!'

Lyrically, the album would differ vastly from its predecessor, something that Caleb attributed to a little inspiration provided by prescription medication. A punch-up between himself and Nathan at their shared Nashville house left the former requiring surgery on a dislocated shoulder and, since this was a problem Caleb had been suffering from for some time, the brotherly bust-up proved the last straw.

'Caleb's always been double-jointed,' Nathan later recalled, 'and it got to the point where his shoulder kept popping out all the time because the tendons were worn down. Then we had a drunken brawl one night and I guess

I just finished the job. He went a whole year and a half where his shoulder would pop out five or six times a day. He couldn't swim, he couldn't ride a roller coaster – all the things we liked doing.'

The fight had occurred in the studio and left the singer with a damaged arm and his older brother with injuries – yet both claimed they couldn't remember exactly why they were scrapping. The fisticuffs became so violent that an assistant cleared the room so the siblings could get physical. 'We still don't know [why it started],' Caleb told *Rolling Stone*, admitting 'It was a big one, though. We were really drunk, one of us said something really deep and hurtful and that was it. Our assistant shuffled people out the door when he knew it was about to go down and, once the house cleared, it was like they let two dogs off their chains – we went *crazy*. It was just a good old Wednesday night in Nashville....'

Coincidentally or not, Nathan had recently decided to work on his physique, having been inspired by Queens of the Stone Age drummer Joey Castillo, after the bands had shared 2007 festival stages. 'Their drummer is a gorilla,' Caleb reveals, 'so we'd be going to Nathan "Look what he can do."' His older brother called the singer's bluff, signed up a personal trainer and was soon hitting the skins with simian force.

Meanwhile Caleb, in a cast and with instructions to wear it for nine months, found the pills provided to aid recovery also aided his songwriting. 'I had to take pain meds for my shoulder. I would wake up the next day and you know, it's all a bit of a blur. I would wake up and go in the living room and my songbook would be open... I wouldn't even really remember writing the lyrics and they would usually be pretty, pretty good. I mean, there would obviously be a couple lines that I was like, that was the pills talking....'

When his writing wasn't assisted by a prescription, Caleb offered further insight into process for penning tracks. 'I'm not the kind of guy that cries and stuff like that. Not that that's a good thing. But, you know, after I've had a few drinks and I have a songbook in front of me, a lot of times I'll kind of talk to myself a little bit, you know, and kind of point a finger at myself, and usually that's the most emotion that comes out of me. I'm going to open up one way or the other, but I think it just happens a little quicker when you have something altering you to give you the confidence to do so.'

Warming to his theme, he told *Rolling Stone* magazine: 'I don't know if it was the pills or what, but the melodies were so much stronger than anything I've ever done – it's just really beautiful songs. I know I sound like a fucking cock right now, but this is the first time I've really been proud of myself, track for track.' Wherever the inspiration had come from, the results were likely to be well worth hearing.

One British band in particular had made a big impression on Caleb's appoach to music – and it wasn't the Arctic Monkeys! Radiohead's *In Rainbows*, the first album released on their own label via the Internet, was a fixture on his playlist at home, and he was particularly impressed at how singer Thom Yourke 'sang the ass' off the 'beautiful melodies' it featured.

Caleb further admitted that, in echoes of REM's Michael Stipe, he'd previously gone out of his way to be unintelligible, holding back on his vocals 'to be cool or whatever', with the result that 'people thought I was 50 years old.' Now, he reflected, he was confident enough to take pride in his singing and perform with the confidence he'd shown many years previously when he was a child soprano in church. ''You'll notice it,' he told *New Musical Express*, 'you can actually understand what I'm singing about.'

Nathan believes his brother used to sing 'raspy so people couldn't understand a word' because it was the opposite of how he used to sing 'all good and clean' in church. 'For our fourth record, the time was right for people to actually understand what's being said.'

A reviewer agreed: 'Lead singer and heartthrob Caleb Followill enunciates better than he did six years ago, when you could barely decipher his tortured kudzu yelp. (Apparently, dating supermodels is good for your diction.) But the frontman still howls at the moon with all the confidence of a drunkard playing chicken on the train tracks.' And Radiohead's Ed O'Brien agreed even more, calling Kings of Leon 'the greatest band on the planet right now. I don't get jealous when I see other bands but when I see them I think, 'Man, I'd love to be in that band''.'

After the relaxing process of recording in Nashville and the successful results that followed, the Kings made the obvious choice of returning to the Music City's Blackbird Studios. 'We know where we're going at the end of the night,' enthused Caleb about the benefits of working close to home. 'We know what restaurant to go to, or you have the luxury of cooking your own meal or sleeping in your own bed. And I don't know, I think besides the work it really gave us all a desire to get in there every day. But yeah, you know, I think the amount of comfort is evident when you listen to the music.'

The four individuals concerned had matured further away from stage and studio. Nathan was now engaged and Caleb was dating model Lily Aldridge, and this relatively stable background gave the group a different outlook on life that was to be expressed through their songs. Even so, when discussing the recording process, Caleb still quipped to *NME* 'We had to get drunk because we all have girlfriends to go home to and deal with.'

But the Kings' creative edge had not been dulled. And while pain meds may have assisted the writing process, alcohol had aided recording: 'We used the studio like a clubhouse.' Nathan said. 'We'd go in there and get a little work done, and when we'd done enough, we would start drinking. If the drinking got out of hand and we didn't do anything else for the rest of the day, at least we'd got enough done to be productive. When you're in the studio, you need to be focused. You can party when you're finished. If you can have the best of both worlds, why not?'

In June the band announced the title of their fourth album. *Only By The Night* was to be released three months later. Named in reference to a line in Edgar Allan Poe's poem 'Eleonora', the album title would contain five syllables, in line with their previous three releases. The quirk was not lost on the Kings, Jared acknowledging: 'We kind of have a five-syllable theme going on with all of our record titles, so we kind of knew it was gonna be that. But, it just so happened that Caleb and I had been talking about Edgar Allen Poe somehow and we Googled him and looked at one of his poems and it just kind of stood out to us and that was one of the many options we had and it ended up beating everything else out.'

But Jared told *Clash* magazine that the process wasn't quite as straightforward as he'd claimed. 'It took us forever to come up with the album title. We had probably five or six that ended up in the shortlist, and we thought about it throughout the entire writing of the record, throughout the entire recording, and it was just something about our record...I mean, we kinda like night feeling stuff, you know, even stuff like vampires and *The Lost Boys* and cool stuff like that; we're all into that, so there was just something about *Only By The Night* that just felt edgy and what we thought this record felt like.'

Contrary to predictions, the Kings kept most of their new material under wraps as they headlined Glastonbury 2008. But they showed no fear by opening with 'Crawl', to give fans a preview of things to come. The track would also kick off the as-yet unheard album and remain their live opener thereafter, and remains one of Matthew Followill's favourite songs to play, alongside 'Black Thumbnail'.

A malfunction on the right-hand video screen caused an eerie black strip to fall across the band, making it seem as if their faces were being censored. But it hardly mattered, as they were roared on to victory by a wholly supportive crowd. Towards the end of the set the band unveiled another newly minted creation to the drunken revellers, 'Manhattan'. Caleb told them: 'The people at the BBC asked us not to play any new songs, but we're going to have to ruffle some feathers tonight because it's Glastonbury.' The applause was, quite naturally, bordering on rapturous.

Having made their festival debut at Michael Eavis's famous farm five years earlier, this was something of a crowning moment for the band, and it was one that they made the most of. 'It was pretty special,' Caleb recalled, 'just considering, you know, we feel like we kind of worked our way up, in the UK especially. We started out in the New Band Tent and then we were main support on the Pyramid Stage and then we, we headlined it. And you know it was really nerve-racking but when we finished we felt like we had really not only done it but we felt like we had done it well.'

Glastonbury was always destined to be a triumph. With Jay-Z making his point by showing up and strumming a spur-of-the-moment version of Oasis's 'Wonderwall' (Noel Gallagher having famously slated the festival for booking a rap act) and the Verve's 'ageing acid majesty' (copyright *New Musical Express*) never in doubt, Kings of Leon simply stormed through the gap. The *NME* Glastonbury preview claimed they were 'One astounding performance away from being the world's biggest underground band' – and so it proved. 'When we leave Glasto,' Caleb predicted, 'people will be saying, "Yeah, they kicked it".'

Kings of Leon effectively fulfilled that expectation when their 23-song set lit up the Pyramid Stage on Friday 27 June. The six-figure audience, plus the watching millions on television, were served up a treat. Even the rain relented and offered a break in the downpour, which ensured most people on the site braved the elements and migrated over to bear witness to their set.

The *Guardian* newspaper not only rated the Kings' performance an 8/10 success but also emphasised their one-ness with the audience. 'As they take the briefest of pauses before an encore of the eagerly awaited and lovingly delivered "Knocked Up", it's clear that Kings of Leon have conceded to the inevitable. No band is bigger than the crowd. And this crowd sure loves them.' They concluded that 'a band with a serious amount of ego can still be humbled by their own popularity.'

Going back to headline, Caleb admitted, had been overwhelming. 'That day, I couldn't look anyone in the eye, I was so nervous, but when I walked on stage there was a peace that washed over me. I didn't hear the crowd, just a dead silence. As soon as we started the set it was like, "Wait a second, this may be Glastonbury, the biggest festival in the world – but right now this is a Kings of Leon concert with a huge drunk audience."'

For Jared 'It was an absolute milestone – one of those few moments where we felt we'd really made it.' But it was an even more special occasion for Nathan. 'We flew our Mom over because it was my birthday the night before, which sucked because I couldn't go crazy with the show the next day. But if ever there was a moment to die after a show, that would be the one. Look at the bands who have headlined it in the past and there we were, three brothers and their cousin from Tennessee.'

Another headline set at Ireland's Oxegen Festival two weeks later ensured the band were cooking on all four cylinders for most of the summer. August saw them return to the UK to play Scotland's T in the Park Festival, and although the Verve were nominal headliners the band were undoubtedly the highlight of the day.

They created a landmark moment by introducing the lead single from *Only By The Night*, 'Sex On Fire', to the UK audience, having debuted it to a lukewarm reception at New Jersey's All Points West Festival days earlier. It had already begun to hit the airwaves, and it would go on to become the Kings' most successful song worldwide. 'Sex On Fire' mixed the quartet's new mature sound and advanced production techniques with good old-fashioned racy lyrics, but its controversial nature meant it nearly didn't make the cut.

Caleb told *NME* 'I just had this melody and I didn't know what to say. Then one day I just sang "this sex is on fire" and I laughed. I thought it was terrible, but the rest of the band were like, "it's good, it's got a hook". I was like "fuck off!" but I ended up writing it. There's an element of sex that's expected in our songs so I tried to wrap it all up in one song. If you read the lyrics you'll find it's got some quite visual lyrics in it.

'It's a pretty sexy song actually, but I knew after writing "Sex On Fire", I couldn't write verses about making out, or going to the movie theatre with a girl. I can't believe the label picked it because the lyrics are pretty in-your-face sexual. I think my girlfriend hopes it's based on her. Maybe it is my girlfriend because we've had some good times together... but I'm not really sure.'

Musically, the song's form could be traced back to that fist-fight with Nathan. Caleb had stitches in his shoulder and couldn't hold the guitar as normal, so his left hand was restricted to playing high up the guitar's fretboard. That was where he picked out the now familiar melody of the song. 'If it wasn't for that fight,' he acknowledged to *Mojo* magazine, 'I wouldn't have played my guitar that high up and I wouldn't have written "Sex On Fire"'.

It was the song's hook ('the size of Hampshire', according to the overawed *New Musical Express*) and overtly sexual lyrics that would catapult the track to Number One in the UK upon its release on 5 September, and while it charted at 56 in the *Billboard* Hot 100, it topped the Modern Rock chart in December, after heavy airplay rotation. 'This made Kings of Leon the biggest band in the world at the moment', said *NME* – and there weren't many who were prepared to argue the point.

The album's big production values and mainstream potential was reflected in the video to the lead single. The band didn't so much stray as totally depart from the straight-shooting performance video, instead producing a different result from anything that Kings fans had seen before – with Caleb writhing around on a bed and Nathan posing topless and doused in water. There were even chickens, with Matthew eating one!

Caleb admitted it was a real departure for the Kings, and was the product of a conversation between him and director Sophie Muller, the British video director whose clients had included Gwen Stefani, Beyoncé and Maroon 5. 'She doesn't really put things on paper, she just goes with what hits her. She told us about the concept and I said it'd be kinda hard to get certain members of this band to do any acting, so she said "Well just stare over into the distance" and I said "The only time you're gonna get Mat to do that is if someone's got a chicken wing on their shoulder!" She ran with it and by the end we were chasing chicken and he was eating chicken. It's his favourite video, I think!'

The single whetted the appetite for the album, and that duly followed on 23 September in the UK and a day later in the US. *Only By The Night* would be final plank in Kings of Leon's world domination platform. And it would cast its net wider for inspiration than had any of its predecessors.

'It's kinda a departure from everything being really personal,' Caleb said of the album. 'We just wanted to write some stories, so there's a lot of different subject matters and a lot of different characters on the album. It's really bass and drum driven, but the melody's still there.' Hopes were high that the glossily-produced, arena-rock 'story' would be successful.

It was immediately clear that the heavy focus on building the production techniques had paid off. The first track, 'Closer', opens with Matthew experimenting with his guitar and effects – creating an eerie and ominous feel – and Nathan's striking drums. Caleb's voice came on stronger than on any previous efforts, as he declaimed 'She took my heart/I think she took my soul' – the singer describing the song as about 'a lovesick vampire'.

This was Kings of Leon music, but not as we knew it. Indeed, a surprised *Maxim* magazine reckoned the track 'crackles with a hypnotic sci-fi riff more akin to [UK progressive rockers] Yes, leaving you slightly concerned that the boys have gone off in some sort of experimental direction'. *NME* felt it opened the album 'on a decidedly queasy note, off kilter-drums and eerie effects spiraling behind Caleb's creeped-out vampiric lyrics and fevered delivery.'

In fact, the song had its origins in the singer's television viewing habits. He was apt to watch murder mystery shows on late-night television. The singer was a 'psycho [who] really feels as if he loves this woman, so much so that if he can't have her no-one can have her.' It all ends up becoming, in his words, 'a brutal story...in a lot of my slow songs there's a woman in the trunk of my car.' With Jared's treated echo bass and Matthew allegedly howling into his guitar pickup, this was one to make the hairs on the back of your neck stand on end, whatever time of day you heard it.

As with *Because Of The Times*, track two picks things up, with Jared's distorted bass once again the immediate sonic focus. As the Kings kick into the politically-driven tirade 'Crawl', Caleb's medication-fuelled lyrics stand out, singing 'The reds and the whites and abused/The crucified USA'. The attitude in the track was to reflect the sentiment behind it, as Caleb explained to *Uncut* magazine: 'I always knew if I wanted to ever do [a political track], I was going

to do it like Rage Against the Machine — it wasn't going
to be some ballad. If you really believe in something, you
should be able to scream it from a mountain.'

Next up was 'Sex On Fire', a track that in no way meant
to change the world, but its anthemic chorus and sexual
lyrics, mixing current and classic Kings, made it an album
highlight. 'A glorious dollop of classic Kings of Leon
rock' according to one reviewer, it was clearly the prime
candidate for the lead-off single to be taken from *Only By
The Night.* 'It's not exactly a thinker of a song,' Caleb has
said of a track whose nonsensical lyrics were memorably
sent up by British stand-up comedian Michael McIntyre.
'I know for a fact that I've written better songs than that.'
Yet this was the song that somehow caught the global
imagination and made the band world-famous.

The following track 'Use Somebody' was to be the
epitome of the band's quest for foundation-shaking, heartfelt rock. The lighter-waving anthem opens with sprawling
guitars before cutting back to Caleb reflecting 'You know
that I could use somebody/Somebody like you'. From
there it is a cocktail of stunning lyrics and soul-stabbing
guitars, perhaps the album's crowning achievement. The
song's quality showed as the single went in at Number 2
in the UK. Even more impressive a feat was reaching the
Top 5 in the United States. The boys had done it – America
was at last standing up and taking notice, and it was not
hard to see why. 'Use Somebody' was perfect arena rock.
The *Sunday Times* reviewer was probably not the first
and certainly not the last to make parallels with U2's
widescreen sound, even before the track had been selected
as a single.

The video for 'Use Somebody' continued the band's
new attitude for the visual side of their songs. They

retained Sophie Muller as director, and the video even contained a love scene between Caleb and girlfriend Lily Aldridge. It also followed the band in the build-up to a live performance, which was also captured. Nathan recounted that it was 'kinda cool and nerve-wracking in the fact that they filmed us actually preparing for a real show. It was actually cool to watch back and see us in that element – having a camera in the dressing room when you go through your pre-show rituals. The director wanted us to play ["Use Somebody"] as the first song of the encore – she got her one shot at glory.'

Given the tough task of following this early highlight was 'Manhattan', the blend of reverb and underlying picked guitars gave a potentially low-key track a kick, but truth be told this was a mere intermission before the second helping of fist-thumping rock that the Kings had to offer. The following track belied its title by zeroing in on the downside of fun and fame, and would provide yet another highpoint.

'Revelry' began by focusing entirely on Caleb's voice, showcasing his strengh and range and the intensity of the new lyrics, something he was proud to show off. 'Because I felt the songs were so strong, I wanted to take the opportunity to actually sing them and showcase my voice, in a way that I never have before. I always used to feel intimidated and tried to hide what I was saying in case people didn't like my opinions.'

The track was the third single to be released from *Only By The Night* and the band's first of 2009, peaking at Number 29 in the UK in March. It would be the band's ninth Top 40 entry there.

Though the slow-paced track never hits the frantic heights of 'Use Somebody', it was still one of the band's favourite songs, Nathan saying 'It makes me feel sad in a good kind of way. I don't know – melancholy, kind of.' From the sombre tone of 'Revelry' straight into the liberal use of church bells on '17' – courting controversy again singing about a young teenager, yet musically described as 'seventies glam' by *The Sun* newspaper – Kings of Leon were creating the sound they wanted, while still singing about the things they knew about. 'This is the record we've wanted to make for ever and we've done it,' Jared enthused.

'Notion' blasts the album into its last 15 minutes, a song that hit back at anyone that had ever criticised Caleb's band – his family. 'We're all a lot closer, especially compared with the beginning. I used to have an idea of how things should go and didn't let other people's opinions matter to me. All that did was hurt our relationship and it took a little while [for the media] to gain the band's trust,' he said.

Nathan pushed the track forward with his drumming. He never overpowers the album, but provides the backbone that holds the record together. The supplementary sound of piano in the chorus simply adds another dimension to the Kings' style, proving they were not afraid to explore new areas. The song was released as a single in June 2009 but disappointingly charted outside the Top 100 in the UK. It fared somewhat better in the US, reaching Number 7 in the *Billboard* Hot Alternative Tracks chart.

The video for 'Notion' completed the band's production journey from their first video for 'Molly's Chambers'. It served as evidence of how the band had evolved both musically and visually in six years. The video was full of special effects and CGI (computer generated images) – including the room the band were playing in crumbling down to reveal a fiery background as they continued playing unfazed – illustrating how the Kings' budget had widely expanded. They meant big bucks now, and everything they were doing was proving it.

As the album winds down, Jared and Nathan combine for the intro to 'I Want You': a laid-back love song in its most basic form. Drum and bass take centre stage, with Caleb's lyrics again making it one of his favourites. 'I like it because it's one of the most simple lyrics that I've ever written, but you know in a way it feels like a big song and when people hear it that's one of their favourites. [Before] I wouldn't have written a lyric like that in the chorus because I would have thought it was cliché. But it feels classic. I didn't over-think it and the music was awesome.'

Nathan's rolling drums kick off the album's penultimate track 'Be Somebody'. The verses contained a menacing undercurrent, Caleb warning 'Now it's your time and you know where you stand/With a gun in your hand'. If this album was indeed inspired, as one reviewer put it, by 'the painkiller-fuelled comedown following a bust-up between Caleb and Nathan', then there was still some spite left in the tale.

Only By The Night closes in much the same way as *Because Of The Times'*. 'Cold Desert' is a slow, desolate expanse of rock riffs and reverberating guitars. *The Sunday Times* felt this 'takes the group's blues roots as its base but makes out of them something almost ambient and totally devastating'. Kings of Leon certainly wanted their fans to go away thinking, rather than merely tired and sweaty from dancing around.

The album received an altogether positive reaction, though not as extravagant as 18 months previously. Had the Kings rushed out their record? 'Whether or not our fans are ready, we just felt like if we don't record it now we're never going to, so let's go ahead and try it. Then, when we put the new stuff up to the other songs, they fit and it didn't feel forced,' Caleb said.

The BBC hailed it as 'The album that the world's been waiting for the Kings Of Leon to make', explaining, 'in the context of a career arc, this level of creativity makes perfect sense. Their sound has had a good five years to grow from post-adolescent indie to full-blown, manly stadium glory.'

However, some critics were less than happy with the Kings' fourth effort. UK championers *NME* also dished a lukewarm reaction to the LP. 'Sad as it is to relate, the Kings have once again made only half of the album of the year. Of course *Only By The Night* will still make them massive. As they gaze upon megaplex after enormodome this autumn, though, they'll have to content themselves with the knowledge they're merely one of the best bands of our times. True immortality – that's been postponed.'

Their other long-time admirers, *Rolling Stone* magazine, also remained unconvinced. 'The revamped sound doesn't always work: cuts like the slow-burning murk-fest 'Cold Desert" feel like sub-John Mayer soul – bland and overly ponderous.' Another critic went further, pondering, 'Has the fire in Kings of Leon's collective belly finally been extinguished? Their fourth album would certainly suggest that the embers are barely glowing.' Trendy music magazine *Blender* could only muster three-and-a-half stars for *Only By The Night*,

The band refuted such allegations, Matthew stating they were simply evolving. 'If you're going to stay recent, you have to change. You can't ever really stay the same. That's just the way we've felt – we have to change with the times. We have found our sound, but we'll still try to spice it up and make things different.'

New Zealand website *Stuff* also gave the US media a dressing-down, saying: 'Keep saying no, America. The rest of the world will gladly have the Kings of Leon. Caleb Followill's indecipherable Southern drawl has been replaced by a slower, more pronounced lilt that sounds like he cares. They're also writing songs that are capable of rocking stadiums and the charts. If you want anthems, *Only By The Night* has got them....'

In contrast to the first two albums, where mainstream success was sacrificed for critical acclaim, the album jetted straight to Number 1 in the UK, and finally pushed through the glass ceiling of the *Billboard* album chart, powering to Number 5 and inserting the Kings firmly into popular US consciousness.

Even before the album was released, however, the band's US stock had been on the rise, capped by their very own appearance on TV's *Saturday Night Live* a week before the LP's launch in September 2008. The band played on the legendary US sketch show, appearing alongside celebrities such as Cameron Diaz. It was a long-awaited accolade and confirmation of their ascent to *bona fide* American sweetheart status.

Nathan explained how the band took their new-found fame with a pinch of salt: '[Country superstar] Keith Urban is a fan, and during our last record, he was in the studio next door, so we got to hang out with him [and actress wife Nicole Kidman]. My fiancée thinks they're best friends now, it's hilarious. She's always like, "Call Nicole and Keith and let's go have dinner." Kirsten Dunst and Johnny Borrell came to one of our shows too. We'd met Johnny before, I think we played a couple of festivals with them. But I've never talked to Kirsten. There's a rule – if a guy in a band brings an actress girlfriend to your show, you can only talk to the guy. It keeps the fistfights to a minimum.'

Not ones to rest on their laurels, the Kings already had an American tour in place to promote the new albums, and set off in October to play over 20 dates everywhere from Las Vegas to home-town Nashville. Caleb spoke of his pride at Kings of Leon's shows, having always believed they were first and foremost a live band. 'We used to be so nervous, but now we're really comfortable on stage. We've got a light show. We're playing bigger places, and we have a lot more songs. We spread the set list out over the four records. You play so much you're going to get comfortable doing this stuff. Our live show is better than ever, and it's only going to get better. Our live show might be the thing that we're most proud of.'

It was just prior to this jaunt and riding high on the album's success that the Kings announced a mammoth show, the first of many that would become commonplace – they would play Madison Square Garden at the start of 2009. If the *Saturday Night Live* appearance was a personal triumph for the band breaking through in America, then this date at the self-proclaimed 'World's Most Famous Arena' was the emphatic rubber-stamp proving that the boys from Tennessee had arrived.

'There's a drastic difference now when we play in the States than there was on the first two records,' said Nathan of the transition. 'We'd come home from playing to 80,000 kids in Glastonbury and arrive back at the airport where our Mom was the only person that knew us! People used to laugh at us with our tight pants and moustaches, but it's got to the point now where we're playing some big, big venues we'd never dreamed of playing at, let alone headlining.'

Caleb concurred in similarly modest tone: ' I don't
think we ever expected, and we still don't expect, to be
playing Madison Square Garden every time we play
New York. We just kind of wanted to spend more time
in America, and it's hard when your success is bigger in
Europe. You spend more time there, and for us, I think
we're just a little homesick. The more that people know
about us here, the more our demand will be.'

But Kings of Leon were part of the musical furniture
in Europe already, announcing their first round of arena
tours during the summer of 2008, setting out in December
and visiting the largest venues Britain's cities had to offer.
From Nottingham's Trent FM Arena to a final date at
Wembley Arena via London's O2, this brought the curtain
down on an amazing year for the Kings.

Writer Tim De Lisle, who attended the Nottingham gig
for the *Mail On Sunday* newspaper, was impressed how
'they hit the ground running and keep up the pace for
two hours, packing in 27 songs and drawing breath only
to thank the crowd, repeatedly, for "all you've done for
us".' He singled out 'Closer', the new album's opening
track that also opened the concerts: '...not much more
than a hypnotic rhythm riff, spreading to the guitars with a
haunting vocal on top from Caleb – and it's excellent.'

He also reckoned there were dull moments where
'Caleb's voice strains to hold it all together'. Perhaps
this was 'Cold Desert', singled out by another reviewer
as 'more like cold sick as it drags on in search of a tune.'
The boys had also been to the barber, with only Nathan
still 'looking the part'. As De Lisle put it, 'the other three
could be in a British indie band – until you hear them
play.' They were, he concluded, 'as American as fried

chicken', and were one of the few American bands selling records (and concert tickets) in reasonable quantities in 2009. White Stripes, the Strokes, REM and Gnarls Barkley just bobbed in their wake.

After the band had reached many new fans when opening for U2 on the first leg of the Vertigo Tour in the US in 2005, it emerged that the Irish megaband were planning a surprise appearance at the O2 in Dublin (formerly the Point Theatre) – as Kings of Leon's support act. Remember, the suggestion had been made to Jared while the tour was happening – but no-one could have thought it might happen so soon. U2 had been approached about staging a full show at the venue, but opted for a series of outdoor shows at Croke Park instead. The Kings meanwhile had been selected to re-open the venue under its new identity, despite local feeling that an Irish band should have been accorded that honour.

Though the first act to perform a ticketed performance at the old Point had been the long-forgotten Huey Lewis and the News, U2 could claim to have been the first act to perform, as they held studio rehearsals for their live *Rattle And Hum* album there in 1988, before it opened to the public as a venue. In the end, the honour of being the first concert in the new O2 went to a multi-artist event for the Childline charity, starring the likes of Anastacia and Enrique Iglesias.

Even so, Bono and his pals were still anxious to be one of the first acts to experience the newly renamed and refurbished venue, so they reportedly approached Kings of Leon to appear as their support act at their 19 December show. It would have been the first time in 25 years U2 had supported anyone.

'There have been serious talks about this happening,'

a source close to U2 revealed. 'The plan was for Kings of Leon to announce they would be joined by a special support act in the run up to the gig. Then before the show Bono and the boys would storm onto stage and perform material from their new album. They would then rejoin Kings of Leon during the show. It will be a monumental rock moment and certainly one of the most unexpected things the band have ever done.'

The plans came to nothing, possibly because the new material mentioned (which would emerge in 2009 as the *No Line On the Horizon* album) would not be ready in time for the O2 opening, but the fact the story developed at all was an indication of how Kings of Leon's star had soared over the intervening months since their US U2 experience. And Bono was snapped leaving the backstage area after the show, having stopped by to present his compliments.

Nor was the touring scheduled to stop any time soon. In a testament to their work ethic, the Kings had already announced a second round of stadium dates for the summer of 2009. 'We've figured out the formula,' Caleb said. 'The harder you work, the more successful you get.' He added the band saw the bigger venues as a way to give back to the fans who had been supporting them from the beginning, but also a way to convert new Followill followers hooked in by their made-for-radio hooks. 'When you get an opportunity to play the O2 in London you have to realise that there will people who have never seen us before,' he says. 'There are two types of people – 'Sex On Fire' fans and Kings of Leon fans. A lot of people only know us from that single, but it's great the tour sold out before it was released.'

The band had followed their Glastonbury triumph with a one-off London show at the Brixton Academy. It was

scheduled on the eve of their appearances at the sold-out
V Festivals as they continued their journey around the
circuit. There were no pre-gig nerves apparent on this
occasion as, having succeeded in fulfilling their aims at
Glasto, the pressure was off. Any tension there was was
broken by a series of illusions from a magician, Dynamo,
they'd met when appearing on the Jonathan Ross TV show.
He was now a regular backstage presence on their visits to
the capital, entertaining the Kings at their London shows.

And there would be yet another memorable one, at the
O2 Arena on 11 December. 'I had a massive smile on my
face, and ever since then I've had a grin' said Caleb. It had
finally sunk in exactly how big Kings of Leon now were.
As the New Year approached the end of 2008, awards
began to flood in, with *Only By The Night* announced
as the third best-selling UK album of the previous year
behind Duffy's *Rockferry* and Take That's *The Circus*.
Indeed, it was one of the fastest-selling records of the year,
the figure of more than 220,000 sold in the first week of
release, beaten only by Coldplay's *Viva La Vida, Or Death
And All His Friends*.

In Australia *Only By The Night* outsold all the
competition, including a long-awaited comeback album
from homegrown heroes AC/DC. This despite only being
released in October. It was a precursor to the trophies
that would be stocking the Followills cabinet in the
coming months, as they would be recognised for their
achievements on both sides of the Atlantic.

'Sex On Fire' and *Only By The Night* were to gain yet
more recognition in the following weeks. Both would
become the biggest-selling single and album downloads
in UK history, toppling Leona Lewis' 'Bleeding Love'
and Amy Winehouse's *Back To Black* respectively. The

latter's download success was appreciated by the boys, who champion the format and see their albums as pieces of work to be enjoyed in their entirety.

'When you listen to a [long-playing] record,' Matthew said, 'you should be able to listen to the whole thing without getting bored. That's one of my favourite things to do. There aren't that many bands you can do that with anymore. You're going to get bored and change the song. We're always nervous about that, and we hate that feeling.' So the fact that people were consuming the whole cake rather than piece by piece was particularly satisfying.

Furthering their reputation as the hardest-working band in rock, Kings of Leon continued to tour through spring 2009, entertaining more of their American fans and capitalising on the national exposure they'd received via the Grammy Awards. Mathew and Jared also told the BBC that plans were in motion for the band's fifth studio album, the youngest Followill saying 'The next album that we make, that we're already working on, I can assure you, is one that I'm the most excited about. We haven't really got down to lyrics yet but we have a lot of good stuff.'

The decision to rapidly follow *Because Of The Times* had paid off. The album had proved to be the breakthrough for the band on so many different levels, not least propelling them into the hearts of their fellow Americans. Homes, too. By March 2009, sales in the States had passed the 500,000 mark.

Nathan reflected on their rise to the top. 'If you'd have told us five years ago that we'd be here – three Grammy nominations, sold out Madison Square Garden, played *Saturday Night Live*, and asked "Do you think that would change you?" we'd have said "definitely" because we'd be on such a bigger level, but it hasn't; we're still the same assholes we were three years ago!'

One thing that had slowed down somewhat with the onset of fame was the rock'n'roll lifestyle. 'You actually party much more like a rock star before anybody knows who you are,' Jared told *Spin* magazine. 'Once people know who you are, you become sheltered by everybody that works for you, you know? It's all roped off little areas where we're the only people there. Us and the strippers.'

'We used to be crazy,' Caleb contributed. 'You could tell by our outward appearance... We used to look the part. We were a band that dreamed of being a rock'n'roll band, and so we were going out, falling off of tables and getting crazy. Now usually it's us and the opening band, and we play pool and drink spritzers....'

Responsibly enjoying the fruits of their labour while still settled in their home town of Nashville, the Kings were branching out, while not forgetting their roots. Caleb summed it up with typical Kings' tongue-in-cheek humour when he quipped 'We gave up critical acclaim, and now we sell records!'

CHAPTER SEVEN

DIVINE RIGHT OF KINGS

So what might the future hold for the four God-fearing boys from Tennessee? It has, by any standards, been a meteoric rise from anonymity to worldwide superstardom – one they could not possibly have foreseen even in their wildest pipedreams. Ever since their triumphant third appearance at Glastonbury in the summer of 2008 life had, in Caleb Followill's words, been 'a fucking whirlwind'.

It seemed everyone wanted a piece of them, and they had done their best to fulfil that demand. But would they pay a price? Every night out has its hangover, and July 2009 found at least one King of Leon nursing a sore head. Worse, far worse was the fact that he'd taken out his frustrations on an iconic item that had played a major role in the band's musical history.

Caleb Followill claimed it was stress that had led him to destroy the beloved 1972 Gibson ES-325 guitar he'd played on almost all the Kings' hits at the end of the band's T In The Park set in Scotland earlier in the month.

It had been their third consecutive appearance at the Scottish festival which they first graced in 2003, and had started well. The Kings took to the stage as the headlining act at the annual music event on Friday 10 July and made an immediate impact. Caleb shouted to the crowd, 'This is one of the festivals that we look forward to the most. We're home, right? We love you guys very much. We love you because you guys have made us... Kings of Leon. And guess what – we're gonna be here forever.'

The singer then made it clear why he was such a fan of the Kinross-based festival... because the Scots are famous for enjoying a drink. He told the packed audience 'If there's anywhere where it isn't frowned upon to drink, it's here, right?' But sound problems led to a rapid change of mood, and the performance almost ended in blows. According to *The Sun* newspaper, a serious backstage fight was only narrowly averted when the band's tour manager dragged the singer away from Nathan, Jared and Matthew.

The singer had taken his frustration out on his beloved Gibson, smashing it as the set finished and casting its broken remains into the crowd. It was unexpected, the more so because Caleb's relationship with Lily Aldridge, publicly displayed if not consummated by their canoodling on the video clip for 'Use Somebody' in late 2008, had appeared to calm him down more than somewhat over recent months.

A source at the festival told the paper: 'He was livid about the sound and took out his anger on stage without considering the consequences. His guitar is now ruined. The crowd were oblivious to the sound difficulties but the Kings want every show to be perfect. When they came off stage, tempers flared and they were effing and blinding at each other. It was really nasty before their tour manager stepped in.'

Apparently, the following night's show at the Oxegen festival just outside Dublin was under threat, but the date was fulfilled – although, of course, Caleb's Gibson didn't make the journey. It wasn't the first such incident of the year, similar fiery scenes having been witnessed at the 2009 Brit Awards.

The guitar would certainly be a big loss. In the words of one magazine, it was 'a stunning workhorse instrument that bears the unmistakable marks of the singer-guitarist's ferocious, percussive style of strumming.' Guitar technician 'Nacho' Followill, the boys' cousin, had previously commented that if anything happened to that guitar, he'd 'just pack up and head home, it was that special.'

Speaking to the Scottish *Daily Record* newspaper after the gig, Caleb explained his actions: 'I got a bit angry and broke my guitar, so I have to get a new one. We have zero reasons to complain, but I do blame me breaking my guitar on being overworked. I would never, ever dream of doing anything to that guitar. It's moments like that where you realise you need a break.'

But with thousands of record-company jobs and the balance sheets of tour promoters depending on them, a break was never likely to be an option. Despite the star's wishes, the group were scheduled to start a 30-date tour of North America on 7 August, with the Whigs as opening act. Then they would fly back to Britain from Los Angeles for a headline appearance at the Reading Festival late in the month. They'd also play the related Leeds Festival the same weekend, before resuming American activities in Maryland on 8 September.

The tour would climax in their home town of Nashville

on 16 October, at which point one could only hope their
diary between then and Christmas had been left as white
as the driven snow. 'Don't get me wrong,' Caleb added.
'We're definitely enjoying it. I think insecurity drives
us to always be better.' Then, with a twinkle in his eye,
he claimed that they 'trying to set new goals. I'm kind of
embarrassed to say them. They probably involve yachts....'

This vaulting ambition didn't prevent the Kings from
showing their more charitable side when, in March
2009, they agreed to headline a major benefit concerts in
Melbourne, Australia, for victims of the country's recent
bush fires. Coldplay headlined a parallel concert in Sydney
which, like the simultaneously-staged Melbourne show,
featured an all-star line-up of domestic and international
acts in imitation of 1985's Live Aid. Indeed, a number of
acts (though not the Kings) flew from one city to another
to appear on both stages.

An interesting sidelight of the Victorian Bushfire Crisis
Sound Relief concerts was the return of politician Peter
Garrett to the microphone with eighties band Midnight
Oil, while iconic Australian act Hunters and Collectors
reformed for the Melbourne event. This wasn't the Kings'
first such show by any means: they'd been pleased to play
a benefit for the University of Chicago's Comer Children's
Hospital earlier in the year.

In interviews, the band were keen to suggest they were
reformed characters, and that much of their fighting and
hellraising was in the past. Jared, still only 22, claimed in
late 2008 that they'd 'all calmed down. I would say that
most of us drink as much as we used to but we don't party
as much. It's become more like hidden drinking.' Nathan
confirmed that 'we've learned to keep what we do a little
more private. At first, it was all about the sex and drugs

and rock 'n' roll. It was great, it got us in the tabloids and got us noticed.

'We used to come to London and stay in little hotels. We didn't want a hotel with a good bar because we wanted to go out and get trashed and be seen. But then we thought, "Do we really want to be socialites?" It started fucking with our creativity. It got to the point where we had become a rock band that was known for everything but music, like actors or actresses that are known for being on the scene but you can't name one good movie they've been in.

'Now we'll stay in hotels that have a cool bar, have a few drinks then pop back to our rooms without making fools of ourselves.' As events would soon prove, however, there was still plenty of smoke coming from this particular fire. And as their UK tour loomed in November 2008, *The Sun* reported further trouble brewing in the Kings of Leon camp.

After telling the newspaper's showbiz reporter Gordon Smart earlier in the year that they were putting the brakes on their over-the-top lifestyle, Smart revealed that tensions within the band were high – and the cause was Caleb's drinking. Things had come to a head a couple of weeks earlier, he claimed, with 'an almighty row and the boys trading blows'. Nathan, Jared and Matthew hadn't spoken to Caleb since, and this had sent record-label bosses into a panic with the tour due to kick off in Brighton imminently.

A source said: 'The others have warned Caleb over and over again that they weren't happy about his drinking but he carried on regardless. The lads have always fought, but they usually sort it out the next morning. Things are completely different this time. The label is deeply concerned that if they don't sort out their differences the tour won't go ahead.'

Jared had reportedly revealed the band's drunken fights could get so bad the security guards employed to protect them from over-zealous fans actually had to separate them. 'We wouldn't have security guards if it wasn't for Caleb. More than anything they protect us from each other. The only time we fight is when Caleb's drunker than he's ever been, so it's not really him. He wakes up and doesn't remember any of it.'

Caleb had in the past admitted to getting so wasted he turned into his drunken alter ego 'The Rooster'. He said: "I hate it man, whenever the word "Rooster" is involved, you can wake me up and I think life is great and have zero memory of what happened.' His nickname was gained because of a supposed likeness to John Wayne's hard-drinking screen cowboy character Rooster Cogburn.

In reality, his role model had been his grandfather, who would 'drink whiskey and do crazy shit... grandpa was the same way (as me).' But he also pointed to country veteran Merle Haggard as a man who 'drank, had woman problems and the whole time kept making music that was sweeter and sweeter.' The music was indeed at a peak, but success seemed only to have fanned the flames of conflict within the ranks.

In February 2009 Kings of Leon did what would have been considered unthinkable two years previously by winning a Grammy for 'Sex On Fire'. The award – 'Best Rock Performance by a Duo or Group With Vocals' – a typical mouthful from the equally elaborately named National Academy of Performing Arts and Sciences – was illustrative of the Kings' meteoric rise. It was clear the Followill family mantelpiece would have to be large to accommodate all the wards they would be picking up in the future – or maybe a new wing could be built?

The band was amused that the honour came for a song that nearly wasn't considered for the album. 'As songwriters we've tackled a lot of different things – politics and religion,' Nathan told the *Daily Mirror*. 'Then we write a song called "Sex On Fire" and it's Grammy-nominated. Of all the songs I've put my heart into, that wouldn't even be in the Top 10.'

Caleb believed that producing an album that was easily accessible to the American masses was the main factor in the band's recent US success. 'I think some of the past work we've done should have been nominated, but because I think we were always doing something kinda different than was what going on out there, this album is a little bit more mainstream, a little easier for people to swallow.'

The band's love affair with the United Kingdom continued ten days later when they won Best International Group and Best International Album at the Brit Awards. They also performed 'Use Somebody' live, which helped ensure *Only By The Night* enjoyed one of its two single-week stints as the UK's Number 1 album directly after the appearance.

The band had fended off competition from the likes of the Killers and AC/DC to pick up the Best International Group Brit while *Only By The Night* beat those same opponents' latest offerings to be acclaimed Best International Album. Caleb spoke fondly, if somewhat ironically, of the Brits before the event: 'We always knew the Brits was the Grammies of the UK. So we basically knew that was our Grammy. It was always the biggest shot that we had. And I hear the gift bags are much better at the Brits. It will be fun to perform. Playing a concert is one

thing but performing in front of loads of jaded artists
is different.'

But the Brits would chiefly be remembered within the
band for significant after-show differences in the ranks.
A showbiz website reported 'a massive bust-up backstage,
prompting a 20-person brawl. Witnesses say the fight
was sparked after Jared Followill's girlfriend saw him
speaking to a female member of British pop star Alesha
Dixon's group. Jared's lover threw water over the sexy
[sic] musician in a fit of jealousy. Other reports say Jared's
bandmate cousin, guitarist Matthew Followill, was jealous
as he was getting less female attention than the other
members, and started the fight with lead singer Caleb Followill.

A source told Britain's *Sun* newspaper: 'Matthew's
always the last one to be asked for an autograph. He hasn't
been feeling part of things, especially at big events like the
Brits. Caleb was annoying him all night, unintentionally, and
all of a sudden something snapped and they just went for each
other. It was like a proper old fashioned bar-room brawl.'

An onlooker said: 'Jared's girlfriend was not happy. She
went ballistic and the next minute more than 20 people
had all piled into the bust-up. It was comical seeing little
Nicole Appleton wading in to try and keep the peace.
Alesha kept out of the way, but (All Saints') Mel Blatt
thought it was hilarious.'

Another insider added: 'The lads had been tucking into
the free booze and things got a bit lairy. They are known
for having fiery relationships with their girlfriends and with
each other. It wasn't surprising there was a bit of a scrap.'

Earlier the Kings had reportedly unleashed a 'foul-
mouthed tirade' when they discovered they were to be
interviewed by the air-headed Fearne Cotton for ITV. They
pulled out at the last minute, screaming: 'What the fuck?

We didn't agree to do this! We're not doing it! We're off! Fuck off!' Fortunately, boxer Joe Calzaghe, a celebrity guest at the event, stepped in to calm things down.

Kings of Leon had successfully put on a show of unity in front of the cameras as they collected their awards – and did so again when they were later spotted in a famous London club, the Met Bar, but significantly without Matthew. The website continued: 'Caleb reportedly went to bed early, retiring just after midnight. However, Jared spent the rest of his night fending off beautiful admirers, saying: "What is it with London? All night I've had a non-stop stream of blonde girls coming up to me and I just want to go to bed."'

With each single release, television appearance and awards ceremony the sales of album four – and the remaining back catalogue – continued to soar. In July 2009 *Only By The Night* was certified platinum in the United States by the RIAA for selling one million copies in the nine months since its release. It was already clear Kings of Leon's fifth studio album, when it came, would have as much to live up to commercially as it did creatively.

This next release was expected in 2010 and even before a note had been committed to tape (or perhaps now hard drive?) was already likely to be one of the releases of the year. Back in January 2009, just before the Kings headlined a sold-out gig at America's most famous arena, Madison Square Garden, Nathan had teased *Rolling Stone* magazine by suggesting there would soon be an album of remixes of Kings tunes.

Their next studio record, which he claimed they hoped to start in November, would be 'a straight gospel album,' he said. But even if this were true, would the band be around to record it or, after that, promote it?

The record company was taking no chances. Just in case
the Kings were shooting stars destined to burn brightly
and explode rather than dazzle forever, they decided to
educate latecomers to the story by jamming the band's first
three albums together in one functional package. *Boxed*
contained no bonus tracks, live versions or outtakes, just
the trio of discs in a slipcase. But as *Short List* magazine
helpfully explained, it 'highlighted the band's progression
from loose Southern-rock jams to full-on stadium-rock epics'
– as well as adding to Sony BMG's already groaning coffers.

The track record of 'family bands' varies wildly, but
is rarely straightforward and harmonious. The obvious
parallel to the Kings was British beat legends the Kinks.
With singer Ray Davies also the major songwriter, lead
guitarist brother Dave was always playing second banana –
the fact that he played the riffs on the historic 'You Really
Got Me', 'All Day And All Of The Night' and other rock
classics was little consolation when big brother took all the
credits and royalties.

Formed in the late sixties, the Allman Brothers were
perhaps the quintessential Southern rock band based
on the partnership of guitarist Duane and keyboardist/
singer Gregg. Their partnership was rocky at times, both
believing they were the leader of the band and should be
recognised as such. Sadly, the argument was solved very
finally by Duane's death in a 1971 motorbike accident.
The Black Crowes suffered similarly, though leaders Chris
and Rich Robinson were at least alive to be able to bury
the hatchet when they reformed in the current decade. In
1994, at the height of their fame, they were barely speaking
to each other and, despite a career filled with multi-platinum
sales, they couldn't even sit in the same room.

Even as gentle a band as the Bee Gees suffered from

sibling rivalry over the years. Like the Kings, the Bee Gees included three brothers, the Gibbs, and certainly two out of the three fancied being the top dog. Robin quit and made a solo album, but had to accept that it was the Bee Gees name that pulled in the punters and soon rejoined.

The most recent and obvious example of a dysfunctional musical family, of course, was Oasis. The Gallagher brothers, guitarist Noel and singer Liam, were well-known to Kings of Leon, who'd shared bills with them on the festival circuit over the years. While they stayed together until 2009, they'd endured more than their share of backstage fisticuffs and tours of the States (1996) and Europe (2000) were interrupted by the departure of Noel, seemingly unable to stomach the behaviour of his brother.

So would the Followills make it through? Would blood prove thicker than water – or would sibling rivalry set in and family familiarity breed contempt? The Gallaghers' personal lives had brought yet more strife, with Noel and Liam's first marriages to 'rock chick' socialite Meg Mathews and singer/actress Patsy Kensit respectively ending in very public disarray.

When band members acquire partners, the camaraderie, and then the music, often suffers. As long ago as July 2007, Nathan's proposal to girlfriend Jessie Baylin had sparked worries among the other members – particularly Caleb – about the band's future. Nathan had popped the question during dinner at a restaurant in New York. But the announcement sparked doubts in the band about their future. 'If he doesn't get a pre-nuptial agreement, he's an idiot,' brother Caleb told *The Independent*. 'Me and him have a lot invested in each other,' he continued. 'We started this band. We bought land and houses together.

We've been best friends since we were little biddy boys.
I don't want him to make mistakes.

'We have friends in bands who are married and their
songs start being watered down because they're all about
the same girl.'

Nathan countered his brother's comments by saying:
'Look at Bono – he's been married his whole career. It's
different for me than it is for Caleb, I'm pushing 30. It's
always hard when big brother starts devoting time to a girl
that would normally be devoted to little brother.'

In 2009, the boot was on the other foot and little brother
was getting all the media attention, like it or not. Caleb
and Lily Aldridge were now fair game for the paparazzi,
their every off-stage move stalked by magazines and
celebrity web-sites. They were pictured hand in hand
strolling through Sydney as the Kings played an Australian
arena tour in March, though Caleb – jauntily sporting a straw
Panama in the pictures – also made time on the trip to play
poker with his band and *High School Musical* star Zac Efron.

Among the many women prepared to pledge their love
for the brothers was British singer Lily Allen. She met one
of the band's management team after performing in the
US and gushingly protested her fandom. She pestered him
to call one of the band — and then told the lucky man: 'I
love you. I want to marry you.' Lily, who later said 'I was
really drunk,' admitted she could not remember which one
she asked! She added: 'We played in Boston on the same
night. I wanted to see them.' Despite the excesses that can
only be imagined should Ms Allen ever hook up with the
Kings, it seemed unlikely Caleb would be trading one Lily
for another any time soon.

Kings of Leon had certainly attracted many celebrated
fans on the way. July 2009 found London band White Lies

giving them their seal of approval, while Radiohead's
Ed O'Brien was another major fan. He likened them
to eighties Liverpudlian new-wavers Echo and the
Bunnymen, and believed they were 'growing, evolving,
they're amazing players.' O'Brien singled out sticksman
Nathan for special praise. 'They're all great but that
drummer is amazing – he's really special.'

Even teen heart-throbs the Jonas Brothers were looking
to the Kings for guidance. 'We're being inspired by some
new music,' said Nick Jonas. 'Kings of Leon is another
big one for us, a lot of different inspirations, a lot of new
sounds. We're just trying to continue to grow as musicians
and songwriters.' Perhaps more credibly, U2's Bono rated
them as his band's competition: 'We see ourselves as
contemporaries of bands like Coldplay, Kings of Leon,
Interpol and even Girls Aloud.' Well, we said *perhaps*
more credibly….

Mark Ronson, hotshot producer of Amy Winehouse
and others, was particularly into the band and had tipped
his hat to them by creating his own version of 'Pistol Of
Fire' from the *Aha Shake Heartbreak* album on his covers
project, *Version*. The admiration was clearly mutual, as the
band had him remix their original track from the master
tapes and paraded the result on the B-side of 'Revelry'
when the track was issued as the third single from *Only By
The Night* in March 2009. It became an instant collector's
item. The same month saw the Kings' tracks 'Crawl',
'Molly's Chambers' and 'Sex On Fire' added to the
computer game *Rock Band* – surely the hottest twenty-first
century barometer of current popularity.

The Kings sold out two shows at London's O2,
formerly the Millennium Dome, where they'd wowed a
sellout crowd the previous December, and scheduled the

following month to be the scene of Michael Jackson's highly unlikely comeback. It would be their biggest show to date. And it would also show exactly how far the other side of the showbiz scales they were from the late, lamented Jacko.

With no stage backdrop and a minimal light show, they barely covered a quarter of the stage area that, a matter of weeks earlier, had hosted the Britney Spears circus of dancers and cheerleaders. Yet despite the seeming unwillingness to make a show, they impressed one newspaper critic who felt the lack of frills 'made their songs all the more powerful and intimate.' That may have between the case with early favourites like 'Red Morning Light', but the unveiling of 'Sex On Fire' gave the male members of the crowd an overdose of testosterone as they hollered along. Blowing the roof off the Dome was no easy achievement, but one the Kings managed without seeming effort.

Argument raged as to whether it was after the fifth or sixth song that Caleb first acknowledged the baying crowd. 'It's good to be home,' he drawled, a shy grin spreading across his bearded features as 'Molly's Chambers' ended. It may have been a Monday night, but 20,000 Londoners were happy to welcome four more adopted cockneys to their number. A third show was added on 30 June and was filmed for future release and Nathan spread the word via social networking site Twitter. 'The show is the big DVD filming at the O2,' he wrote. 'So wear something pretty and get drunk before you get there. Party time.'

Now that the Kings were at a level where they were playing mega-venues like the O2 for consecutive nights, Caleb reasoned, 'you obviously have to switch it up a little.' This meant bringing back old songs that hadn't been played in a while and varying the set so that die-hard fans who invested in tickets for more than one night got their money's worth. He had been apprehensive about delving back into the songbook in this way, but was relieved to find reviving them was 'like riding a bike'.

The old songs, so far at least, have been holding up remarkably well in comparison with the newer pages of the KoL songbook. Indeed, this performance threw up the possibility of a live album being released at some stage. As we've already learned, a DVD was in the works. But as recordings had been made throughout their live career, maybe an anthology covering the decade might be considered.

The live album is the traditional stopgap used when a band has had enough of being on the road, or no stomach for yet another studio album. But a live album could be rather more than that in the Kings' hands. Indeed, bootleg recordings are criss-crossing the globe as we speak, the Internet having made it ridiculously easy for fans to swop their own unofficial recordings.

Live tracks have continued to slip out from under the radar, most notably the curiously-titled 'Day Old Belgian Blues' EP. Reissued in June 2009, the recording had originally been distributed three years earlier with Belgian music magazine *Humo*. The CD, packaged as a limited edition Digipak, consisted of six tracks recorded live at the Ancienne Belgique venue, Brussels, in November 2004. These were 'Taper Jean Girl', 'The Bucket', 'Soft', 'Molly's Chambers', 'Four Kicks ' and 'Trani'. All but 'The Bucket' and 'Trani' were made available in various formats of 2005 singles, while a version of 'Knocked Up' recorded live at Ireland's Oxegen Festival in 2008 backed the 'Sex On Fire' CD single a mere matter of weeks after it was performed.

Interestingly, given his continuing liaison with model girlfriend Lily Aldridge, Caleb revealed to *Q* magazine that he had suffered from image problems when he was a youngster. He would run in extreme temperatures and lived on a diet of coffee, despite not being overweight. 'I always thought that I wasn't good enough,' he said. 'I'd do anything to keep my hands and mouth busy without eating.' Although he admitted he had now overcome his diet problems, he said he was still concerned about his image. 'I want to look like I can defend myself. I want a guy to look at me in a bar and know he can't talk shit to me or run me over – even though he probably could.'

The summer was the festival season and the Kings were, as ever, fully committed. June had been spent playing European arenas in London, Hamburg, Cologne, Berlin, Stuttgart and Luxembourg, but July saw them venturing outdoors. Rock Werchter, Belgium, and the Hultsfred Festival in Sweden were among the triumphs. It was a tribute to the loyalty of the bands fans that they sold out each and every appearance, despite the continuing recession. 'Just because things are going well for us, that doesn't mean we don't have family and friends – that we don't see the effects and what's happening,' declared Caleb. 'Anyone who's going to come and spend that money, I hope they get their bang for their buck!'

But many fans were disappointed when their Benicassim 2009 headline slot was pulled on 17 July, due to extreme weather conditions. Wind and rain lashed the Spanish festival site, causing the removal of the large video screens beside the Escenario Verde stage and pinning down sections that had come loose. The music did kick off, with Paul Weller playing a set on the stage at 9:30pm. But later in the evening the wind got so bad that

the smaller stages were cordoned off. Kings of Leon's
11pm set was initially delayed, with Tom Tom Club
playing instead – only to be greeted with boos from fans
of the Kings. Then at around 1am it was announced that
the band would not be playing as the conditions were
too dangerous.

Organisers had hoped to reschedule the Kings' slot for
the following night, but the band had already departed.
Drummer Nathan Followill wrote on his Twitter page:
'I'm sad to say that we aren't playing Benicassim. We are
so sorry and bummed about last night. Our gear is already
headed to Switzerland.'

There was understandably some negative Internet
comment from those who had been let down. Alyssa B
was one such dissatisfied customer. 'There are no words
to describe how disappointed I am with KoL. I was front
row centre for seven hours. I lined up waiting for the main
stage to open, pushed and shoved, couldn't get out to go to
the loo... which all would have been worth it to see them
play. But they didn't and Tom Tom Club did.

'I know the wind was bad and it was only a matter of
time before they had to close the whole festival down but
if Tom Tom Club came out to play half their set Kings
of Leon could have done the same. What has happened
to you guys? When did you become so precious? Five
years ago you would have done it. Now, with all this new
stardom and glory you put yourself up on some pedestal?
Now you are just like any other mainstream indie band
and to me you have lost your appeal.'

It wasn't the first sign of dissatisfaction. The Oxegen
date in Ireland had been played after T in the Park, and
the band delivered an adequate set. But some fans were
disappointed when, at the end of the concert, the band

walked off without a word, declining to play an encore for which the whole crowd was waiting. Several boos were aimed at the stage. 'I know Kings of Leon are amazing,' said one post to their website, 'but don't let the fame go to your head, after all we are the ones who made you and a little interaction with the crowd doesn't take much effort!'

Looking even further ahead, the Kings would be eligible for induction to the Rock'n'Roll Hall of Fame in 2028. For now, though, they could content themselves on having appeared on the cover of *Rolling Stone*, the old-school benchmark of having 'made it'. 'It's one of those things I'm pretty sure will sink in down the road,' said Caleb.

He was fully aware that the older fans of the band would not see this accolade, coming on the heels of an album one critic called 'a relatively slick departure from its early work, which was violent, disturbing, muddy, chilling', as a career highpoint. 'There are two kinds of people, he explained. 'There are 'Sex On Fire' and 'Use Somebody' fans, and there are long-term Kings of Leon fans. A lot of people only know us from those singles, but we can't afford to treat anyone differently. We still have to play great shows that everyone will love. And that's what we always plan to do.'

Nowadays, Caleb admitted to *Mojo* magazine, he could look out into the crowd and see people 'don't look anything like us and I can tell they don't have the same backgrounds. I see people come to concerts and I think, "Man, what is it that got them there?" I can't pick and choose who relates to the music. I just scratch my head every night.'

It was a similar dilemma that had faced Nirvana's troubled main man Kurt Cobain when his band vaulted to supergroup status over a decade earlier, thanks to the double whammy of *Nevermind* and 'Smells Like Teen Spirit'. Towards the end of his life, Kurt Cobain saw heavy-metal kids and yuppies coming to his shows and he didn't like it. He would get angry that his audience was changing into middle-class, middle-of-the-road listeners, and the idea that Nirvana's music was something his fans could play for their parents drove Cobain crazy.

When asked what he hated most about being famous, Kurt answered: 'Kids with Bryan Adams and Bruce Springsteen T-shirts coming up to me and asking for autographs.' He also hated the band being lumped in with other bands like Pearl Jam, citing another pet hate as 'People in the audience who hold up a sign that says "Even Flow" (a Pearl Jam song) on one side and "Negative Creep" (a Nirvana song) on the other.' At the peak of his popularity, he often wore a T-shirt declaring 'Grunge Is Dead', while posing in make-up and a dress on the cover of style magazine *The Face* appeared to be another attempt to alienate an unwanted section of his fan following.

If popularity was a double-edged sword for Kurt Cobain, it was bandmate Krist Novoselic who put his finger on the problem. 'We've always treated people with that mentality with a little bit of contempt and cynicism,' he said of the 'Guns N'Roses kids' Kurt now saw with dismay were into their music. 'To have them screaming for us...why are they screaming? What do they see in us? They're exactly the same kind of people who wanted to kick our ass in high school.' But you can't pick and choose your audience, particularly when it grew with such unexpected speed, as Kings of Leon were fast finding out.

Caleb's on-stage musings as the Kings played at

summer 2009's Lollapalooza Festival were instructive.
It was their third time playing the annual event, and he
recalled the first: "We'd see ten people and they would see
us dressed up and with our moustaches and leave. Thank
you for making us feel like a much bigger band than we
are!' Yet as he addressed an estimated crowd of more than
100,000, the singer was undoubtedly aware that some of
their original followers felt the group had sold out with the
new, more commercial 'Sex On Fire' sound. 'I know a lot
of fans have lost faith in Kings of Leon,' he said. 'But fuck
it, we're just having a good time.'

The Kings showed a desire to make more of a mark on
the music business than just as songsmiths and performers
when, in June 2009, they announced the launch of a new
record label with independent music publisher Bug Music.
Bug CEO John Rudolph announced the first release on the
imprint would be the Features' 'Some Kind of Salvation',
co-produced by Jacquire King.

Bug Music and the Kings had entered into an
agreement in late 2008 that allowed them to jointly sign
and develop artists. 'Caleb, Jared, Matthew and Nathan
are extraordinary tastemakers and constantly absorbing
new sounds from all over the world,' said Rudolph. 'The
honesty in their music is what draws them to genuine
artists. We are excited about developing new artists
together as Bug Music continues to innovate and challenge
the industry's traditional thinking of a publisher.'

To prove that charity begins at home, the Features were
fellow Tennessee brethren who had previously toured the
UK and US with the band as support in 2007. The band
– Matthew Pelham (guitar, lead vocals), Roger Dabbs
(bass guitar), Mark Bond (keyboards) and Rollum Haas
(drums) – were slated to hit the road throughout the US

that summer in support of the album release.

For all their on-the-road wrangling, the four bandmates had bought homes within a three-block radius of each other in Nashville. 'We have a movie theatre, our favourite bars and restaurants,' said Nathan. 'It's cool.' Caleb believed they were 'all a lot closer, especially compared with the beginning. I used to have an idea of how things should go and didn't let other people's opinions matter to me. All that did was hurt our relationship and it took a little while to gain the band's trust. Now we're a lot stronger. Obviously the work can get to me, and I lash out at the people I love, but we're accomplishing so much more than we ever thought we would.'

As seasoned world travellers, Kings of Leon had been perturbed, as had many Americans during the Bush era, to be perceived as representing a belligerent nation. And while they were by no means a political band, 'Crawl' had suggested the 'crucified USA' had to learn to walk on all fours. Jared saw the song as depicting his country 'losing its global empire'. And Caleb admitted that he was looking forward to a new face in the White House to replace the outgoing Bush – 'we don't even really care who it is'. 'Crawl', incidentally, was obviously a significant song in the Kings' canon – so much so that it was released as a free download on the band's website in July 2008, fully six weeks in advance of the album release.

When it came to flying the American rock flag, the Kings had more or less inherited the standard from the Red Hot Chili Peppers, Foo Fighters and Green Day – the 'big three'. It remained to be seen if they'd make the indelible mark of a Nirvana. But crucially, and unlike Cobain and company, they drew their fans from both sexes.

'They have a big female following, drawn to their

swagger, charisma and air of hairy degeneracy,' gushed the *Guardian* in late 2008. 'They have the double-whammy: a reputation for adhering to rock's sex-and-drugs credo to the letter, as well as a sense that they're in touch with their softer, more spiritual sides. For women who have outgrown Westlife et al, Kings of Leon are the most credible boy-band on the planet, and for the guys, well, they offer simple rock thrills with a hint of danger. What's not to like?'

The Kings had broken through where the likes of the Strokes, whom they'd supported not so long ago, had proved wanting. They'd yet, however, to come up with their definitive *BloodSugarSexMagik*, the Chilis' breakthrough opus. Maybe it was scheduled to be *Only By The Night*, but as one reviewer said 'This is the album that's supposed to be the aural epilogue released after spending ten years at the top of the heap, not the prologue that slips out just before the band was about to get there.'

When the new album passed the half-million mark in the first quarter of 2009, Caleb had said: 'It's not like it is in England quite yet, but that kind of success feels like it is just round the corner.' Their first headlining tour of their homeland had been a 17-date affair, and at the sold-out Spectrum in Philadelphia they were clearly not only on top form but in high spirits. 'I think America is starting to see the light!' proclaimed Caleb in evangelical fashion, to the obvious delight of the 17,000-strong audience.

The band now had a depth of repertoire that enabled them to reel in the audience at will. As one 2009 concert review put it, 'After working its hits early, KoL uncorked a lengthy encore of deep cuts and diehard goodies.' No longer the victim of constant comparison, this was a band at the top of its game. As far as could be ascertained, it seemed the Kings of Leon were here to stay. If they could keep a lid on their simmering sibling rivalry, the new rock royalty was set to rule for some while to come.

POSTSCRIPT

The Kings' headlining appearance at the Reading Festival in August 2009 was supposed to be a crowning achievement, capping a year that had seen them attain global supergroup status. Instead, a worrying re-run of the T in the Park tantrum earlier in the summer demonstrated that tensions remained, and that an uncertain period in the band's career had yet to end.

The set at the weekend event was blighted by a recent sound curfew, compounded with high winds that affected almost every main stage act that weekend. This not only meant that the impact of the music was partially lost in the swirling winds, but also that much of the initially positive audience reaction failed to reach the stage. But there was something more: the boys appeared to have little or no relationship with the tens of thousands who had congregated to see them play.

Old favourites like 'Molly's Chambers' and 'Red Morning Light' were slowed down to fall in line with the Kings' expansive new 'arena' sound, and failed to ignite the crowd in the time-honoured fashion on which they had come to rely. Kings of Leon were apparently trying to re-write their musical history. They seemed to have forgotten that their fans loved their old material the way it was originally played, as an essential accompaniment to the newer songs that were, in many respects, almost public property.

Crowd interaction had never been the Kings' strong point, but despite Caleb pleading with the crowd to get involved in the set, no spark was ignited. This clearly disgruntled the front man, as he proceeded to launch into a tirade at the gathered mass. 'We know you're sick of Kings of Leon. We're fucking sick of Kings of Leon too. But we get up here every night and I thank God for everything I've had. So for all those who don't give a fuck about us, I understand. But we've worked hard to be here. We're the goddam Kings of Leon, so fuck you.'

Perhaps understandably the boys declined to encore, exiting the stage amid more trashing of instruments. With Noel Gallagher choosing the weekend to quit Oasis, the undisputed sibling band of the nineties, the online press were quick to highlight real questions hanging over the immediate future of Kings of Leon. After all, a sizeable US tour stretched ahead of them – and such a jaunt, as Oasis had found in 1996 and '99, could be fraught with tensions.

And within minutes of leaving the Reading stage, the band themselves were pouring fuel on the festival campfire. Nathan posted on Twitter: 'Reading? What the fuck? Zero love for the Kings. I know it was cold but holy shit, y'all were *frozen*. I can only hope Leeds is in better form.' Their loyal English fanbase were appearing to grow weary of the drastic change in style and perceived 'A-list' attitude. In the eyes of much of the Reading crowd, the young, raw family band from Tennessee had changed into celebrity prima donnas with neat haircuts and arty videos.

Interestingly, Caleb had ended an interview in the then-current issue of *Total Guitar* magazine with an appropriate quote. 'The bigger the band get, the more shit we have to deal with. We realise that.'

Having had two days post-Reading to take his own advice, the singer informed the Leeds Festival crowd that the Kings were going to lick their wounds and continue, concluding with the following conciliatory message: 'It was the UK that made us feel like we could take on the world. In the process we may have lost a few fans, but we've got the best fucking fans in the world.'

Had success spoiled Kings of Leon…or was the summer of 2009 merely a hangover ? Time would tell.

A TO Z OF
MUSICAL INFLUENCES

When you've spent your early years away from popular music, the opening of the floodgates is bound to have an effect. Kings of Leon have worn their influences proudly. Here, arranged in alphabetical order, are some of them.

RYAN ADAMS
This former protégé of producer Ethan Johns had a punky, rebellious attitude that he took into modern country music. The Followills must surely have heard and appreciated his output.

ALLMAN BROTHERS
A band from the Deep South who based their appeal on duelling psychedelic guitars, with the occasional soulful vocal thrown in. A way Kings could possibly develop, rather than a past influence.

THE BAND
Guitarist Matthew is a particular disciple of Bob Dylan's erstwhile backing group that cut one of the seminal country-rock-roots albums in 1968's *Music From Big Pink*.

BLACK CROWES
'Fans' and 'The Runner' from *Because Of The Times* remind some listeners of the Robinson brothers' similarly hirsute outfit that cleaned up in the late eighties/early nineties.

BLACK OAK ARKANSAS, THE OZARK MOUNTAIN DAREDEVILS AND THE AMAZING RHYTHM ACES

Seventies Southern rock bands quoted in *Rolling Stone*'s review of *Because Of The Times*… possibly found in their father's record collection?

BRIT-POP AND UK NEW WAVE

The driving guitar riff in 'Charmer' is remarkably similar to Wire's 'Ex Lion Tamer', with a diversion by way of Blur's 'Song 2'.

THE CLASH

It's the attitude as much as the music that gave the band inspiration when they arrived in Joe Strummer's home city of London and were rapturously received.

CREEDENCE CLEARWATER REVIVAL

West Coast blue-collar band of the sixties, who took inspiration from Bayou country. Kings of Leon refer to 'the poor, poor boys' in the chorus of their 'Slow Night, So Long', while John Fogerty sings about Willy and the Poor Boys on 'Down On The Corner'. Coincidence?

BOB DYLAN

Lyrics were never Kings of Leon's strongest suit in the early days, but the likes of 'Knocked Up', which opened third album *Because Of TheTimes* is certainly Springsteen-esque if not Dylan-esque.

AL GREEN

The Reverend Al Green's music formed part of their gospel past where the Followills witnessed church music at first hand as a family.

MERLE HAGGARD

A hellraising country singer from a rather earlier generation, Haggard (most famous songs 'Mama Tried' and 'Okie From Muskogee') has left a mark on Caleb, both lyrically and vocally. They both drink hard too!

JOY DIVISION

Peter Hook's sparse, driving lead bass style has certainly echoed loudly in Jared's playing. 'California Waiting' is an early example of many.

LYNYRD SKYNYRD

It took a plane crash in 1977 to halt the rise of these Southern hellraisers, best known for the bar-band standard 'Sweet Home Alabama'. It's the whiskey-swigging attitude as much as the crackling guitars and underrated song writing that have made an imprint on Kings Of Leon's musical profile. 'Genius' on *Youth And Young Manhood* is just one possibly unconscious homage.

PIXIES

The Kings' third album cut 'Charmer' was either a tribute to or a rip-off of the seminal 'loud/soft' punk outfit, with shades of their epic 'Bone Machine'.

QUEENS OF THE STONE AGE

Touring with this band and observing their all-action sticksman Joey Castillo gave Nathan the incentive to improve his stamina, and the result was a more muscular drum sound on *Only By The Night*. Castillo's predecessor was Dave Grohl... go figure!

RADIOHEAD

A study of Thom Yorke's singing on their *In Rainbows* album inspired Caleb to venture more confidently into the vocal arena, as *Only By The Night* showed.

ROLLING STONES

Older Svengali Angelo Petraglia helped the siblings hone their song writing skills and introduced them to the musical influences of the Rolling Stones in particular. Hear this on the first album's 'Spiral Staircase'.

THE STROKES

On XFM in 2008 the Kings confirmed that the Strokes were 'possibly one of the biggest influences of our band when we were starting out and decided to make a band. They're good friends of ours.' First album cuts 'Happy Alone' and 'Wasted Time' tell the story.

TOMMY JAMES AND THE SHONDELLS

Their catchy bubblegum hit from 1968 'Crimson and Clover' was one of the first pop songs Caleb can recall hearing.

U2

The music of Kings of Leon acquired a new arena dimension after touring with Ireland's finest. This was apparent on the 2007 album *Because Of The Times*, especially its closer, 'Arizona'. Plus you can still hear The Edge on 'Sex On Fire'.

THIN LIZZY

The Irish hard-rockers' debut hit from 1973, a rocked-up traditional 'Whiskey In The Jar', contained a line about 'Molly's Chambers' that clearly resonated with the boys. It was a story about gory murder, too… Matthew is also a big fan of their later-period harmonised lead guitars.

VELVET UNDERGROUND

Another Petraglia favourite introduced to the lads bore fruit with their use of drone sounds and the Lou Reed-esque lyrical imagery of 'Trani'.

TOM WAITS

Not an expected one, this, but the tale of 'Joe's Head' from the band's first album is outlandish enough to have turned up on Waits' *Swordfishtrombones* or another collection of bizarre story songs.

WEEZER, TELEVISION

Disparate new wave and post-new wave US rock bands that comprised some of the Kings' early listening.

NEIL YOUNG

A major favourite of their father, whose fire and brimstone lyrics and apocalyptic guitar solos, not to mention wildman looks, do indeed have a certain biblical quality.

ZZ TOP

The Texan trio were another early love of Matthew's – a band with as much hair as the Kings themselves, and a similar gung-ho attitude. They also adapted and refined their sound and image to find greater commercial success, a process the Kings have followed.

POSTSCRIPT

The Kings are now proving a potent musical influence in their own right. Beth Ditto of the Gossip recently added an acappella 'Sex On Fire' to their set, while another 2008 hit, 'Use Somebody', has attracted live covers from the likes of Paramore, Pixie Lott, VV Brown, Friendly Fires, Nickelback and Bat for Lashes. More than their fair share of girls there....

UK DISCOGRAPHY

With notes detailing selected releases from elsewhere
that might be of interest to the collector.

ALBUMS

Youth And Young Manhood

UK release date: 7 July 2003
Highest UK chart position: 3
US release date 19 August 2003
Highest US chart position: 113

CD
Red Morning Light (2:59)/Happy Alone (3:59)/Wasted Time (2:45)
/Joe's Head (3:21)/Trani (5:01)/California Waiting (3:29)/Spiral
Staircase (2:54)/Molly's Chambers (2:15)/Genius (2:48)/Dusty
(4:20)/Holy Roller Novocaine (4:00)/Talihina Sky* (3:47)
*Hidden track

Hand Me Down HMD27

Double 10-inch vinyl in gatefold sleeve
Side A
Red Morning Light (2:59)/Happy Alone (3:59)/Wasted Time (2:45)

Side B
Joe's Head (3:21)/Trani (5:01)/California Waiting (3:29)
Side C
Spiral Staircase (2:54)/Molly's Chambers (2:15)/Genius (2:48)
Side D
Dusty (4:20)/Holy Roller Novocaine (4:00)

Hand Me Down HMD26

Notable variants
Japanese CD version (BMG BVCP-24058) - includes 'Wicker Chair'
US 11-track promo CD version - comes in a stickered card sleeve
(RCA RADV 52394 2)
The album was re-issued with *Aha Shake Heartbreak* as a 2-for-1
package on 1 August 2008 (RCA 88697 00355 2).

Aha Shake Heartbreak

UK release date: 1 November 2004
Highest UK chart position: 3
US release date 22 February 2005
Highest US chart position: n/a

CD
Slow Night, So Long (3:54)/King Of The Rodeo (2:55)/Taper Jean
Girl (3:05)/Pistol Of Fire (2:20)/Milk (4:00)/The Bucket (2:25)/Soft
(2:59)/Razz (2:15)/Day Old Blues (3:33)/Four Kicks (2:09)/Velvet
Snow (2:11)/Rememo (3:23)/Where Nobody Knows* (2:24)
*Bonus track on later pressings

Hand Me Down HMD39

**Double 10-inch clear vinyl in gatefold sleeve (Numbered
limited edition)**
Double 10-inch black vinyl in gatefold sleeve
Side A
Slow Night, So Long (3:54)/King Of The Rodeo (2:25)
/Taper Jean Girl (3:05)
Side B
Pistol Of Fire (2:20)/Milk (4:00)/The Bucket (2:25)

Side C
Soft (2:59)/Razz (2:15)/Day Old Blues (3:33)
Side D
Four Kicks (2:09)/Velvet Snow (2:11)/Rememo (3:23)

Hand Me Down HMD40

Notable variants
Australian 2-CD Tour Edition (released 16 January 2006) includes
the standard 12-track album and a bonus CD featuring five
numbers, Taper Jean Girl/The Bucket/Soft/Molly's Chambers/Four
Kicks, recorded live in Belgium. (Sony/BMG Australia 82876 76410 2)
An Audiophile 180gm vinyl edition was also released in the US on
the Control Group label (CGO 026)
The album was re-issued with *Youth And Young Manhood* as a
2-for-1 package on 1 August 2008 (RCA 88697 00355 2).

Because Of The Times

UK release date: 2 April 2007
Highest UK chart position: 1
US release date 3April 2007
Highest US chart position: 25

CD
Knocked Up (7:10)/Charmer (2:57)/On Call (3:21)/McFearless
(3:09)/Black Thumbnail (3:59)/My Party (4:10)/True Love Way
(4:02)/Ragoo (3:01)/Fans (3:36)/The Runner (4:16)/Trunk (3:57)
/Camaro (3:06)/Arizona (4:50)

Hand Me Down HMD52

Two bonus tracks were available to those who downloaded
the album from iTunes
In the UK: 'On Call' (AOL Music Sessions) (3:21)
In the US: 'My Third House' (4:03)

(Unlike the first two albums, *Because Of The Times* was not made
available on vinyl in the UK. It has, however, been issued on vinyl in
the US, as detailed below).

Notable variants -
Japanese CD version (BMG BVCP-21524) includes 'My Third House'.
A limited edition audiophile 180gm vinyl edition featuring the 13
tracks that appear on the standard CD version was also released
in the US on the Control Group label (CGO 041 - red vinyl)
US 13-track promo CD version: with different artwork
(Hand Me Down 88697 07741 2)
Australian Tour Edition: includes the standard 13-track album
and a bonus DVD featuring 18 numbers, Black Thumbnail/Taper
Jean Girl/King Of The Rodeo/My Party/Fans/Soft/Arizona/Molly's
Chambers/The Bucket/Milk/Four Kicks/On Call/California Waiting
/Spiral Staircase/Trani/McFearless/Charmer/Slow Night So Long,
recorded live at the Hammersmith Apollo, London, 18th April 2007.
(Hand Me Down HMDS55/88697 20209 2)

Only By The Night

UK release date: 22 September 2008
Highest UK chart position: 1
US release date 23 September 2008
Highest US chart position: 25

CD
Closer (3:57)/Crawl (4:06)/Sex On Fire (3:23)/Use Somebody (3:50)
/Manhattan (3:24)/Revelry (3:21)/Seventeen (3:05)/Notion (3:00)
/I Want You (5:07)/Be Somebody (3:47)/Cold Desert (5:34)

Sony BMG/RCA 88697 35199 2

A bonus track was available to those who downloaded the deluxe
version of the album from iTunes: 'Frontier City' (3:37). This was
also made available on the US audiophile vinyl edition.

UK Tour Edition CD
Features the standard 11-track CD plus a bonus DVD that includes
Use Somebody/On Call/Sex On Fire/Crawl/Manhattan recorded live
in London.

Notable variants
Japanese CD version (BMG BVCP-21631) includes 'Beneath The Surface'.

A limited edition audiophile 180gm vinyl double album edition, featuring the 11 tracks that appear on the standard CD version plus 'Frontier City', was also released in the US on the Control Group label (CGO 053)

Target exclusive edition features the standard CD album plus a bonus disc that includes seven numbers, King Of The Rodeo /Slow Night So Long/Fans/Molly's Chambers/My Party/Arizona/ Charmer, recorded live at the Hammersmith Apollo, London, 18 April 2007 (all previously included on the tour edition of *Because Of The Times*).

Boxed

3 CD Box set that includes the first three albums in a deluxe slipcase featuring new artwork by the same designer that has created all of the Kings Of Leon albums (Sony 88697 54737)

SINGLES

Holy Roller Novocaine
UK release date: 18 February 2003
Highest UK chart position: n/a

3-track CD single (Digipak)
Molly's Chambers (2:16)
California Waiting (alternative version) (3:28)
Holy Roller Novocaine (4:02)
Hand Me Down HMD21

10-inch red vinyl (Numbered limited edition)
Molly's Chambers (2:16)
California Waiting (alternative version) (3:28)
Holy Roller Novocaine (4:02)
Hand Me Down HMD20

Notable variants
Promo 3 track CDR in PVC sleeve including gatefold (No catalogue number)

US exclusive 5-track CD EP in unique digipak picture sleeve: includes two tracks not found on the UK release. Molly's Chambers (2:16)/Wasted Time (alternative version) (2:47)/California Waiting (alternative version) (3:28)/Wicker Chair (3:08)/Holy Roller Novocaine (4:02) (RCA 07863 60614 2)

(The versions of 'California Waiting' and 'Wasted Time' featured on these releases differ from those found on *Youth And Young Manhood*).

What I Saw EP
UK release date: 26 May 2003
Highest UK chart position: n/a

10-inch blue vinyl (Limited edition of 2,000)
Red Morning Light (2:59)
Wicker Chair (3:08)
Hand Me Down HMD22

CD
Red Morning Light (2:59)
Wicker Chair (3:08)
Talihina Sky (3:47)
Hand Me Down HMD23

DVD
Red Morning Light (Audio) (2:59)
Red Morning Light (Video)
Introducing The Band (Parts 1, 2, 3 & 4)
Hand Me Down HMD24

Molly's Chambers
UK release date: 11 August 2003
Highest UK chart position: 23

CD (Digipak)
Molly's Chambers (2:15)
Wasted Time (Live at the Birmingham Academy 27 June 2003)
Spiral Staircase (Live at the Birmingham Academy 27 June 2003)
Hand Me Down HMD29

CD

Molly's Chambers (2:15)
Molly's Chambers (Live at the Birmingham Academy 27 June 2003)
Red Morning Light (Live at the Birmingham Academy 27 June 2003)
Hand Me Down HMD30

10-inch (Limited edition of 6,000)

Molly's Chambers (2:15)
Holy Roller Novocaine (Live at the Birmingham Academy 27 June 2003)
Hand Me Down HMD28

Notable variants

Promo CD single featuring Molly's Chambers/California Waiting
/Holy Roller Novocaine (Hand Me Down PROMO2)
1-Track Promo CDR In Custom Promo Sleeve (Jewel case)
(No catalogue number).
UK BMG Promo Video (1-track PAL promo video: not DVD!!)
(KOLVIMO256232)

Wasted Time

UK release date: 20 October 2003
Highest UK chart position: 51

CD

Wasted Time (2:45)
Molly's Hangover (4:23)
Joe's Head (Live in LA) (3:17)
Wasted Time (Video)
Hand Me Down HMD 32

10-inch silver-grey vinyl (Numbered limited edition)

Wasted Time(2:45)
Molly's Hangover (4:23)
Hand Me Down HMD31

Notable variants -

UK CD-R promo Radio Edit - 1-track promo CD in card cover
with different artwork (Hand Me Down HMD34)

California Waiting
UK release date: 16th February 2004
Highest UK chart position: 61

CD
California Waiting (3:29)
Joe's Head (Live at the Brixton Academy) (3:20)
Hand Me Down HMD35

10-inch clear vinyl (Numbered limited edition of 5,000)
California Waiting (3:29)
Joe's Head (Live at the Brixton Academy) (3:20)
Hand Me Down HMD 36

Notable variants
UK 1-track CD promo in gatefold Digipak with different artwork
(Hand Me Down HMD35)

The Bucket
UK release date: 25 October 2004
Highest UK chart position: 16

7-inch vinyl, P/S
The Bucket (2:55)
Trani (live at the Bonnaroo Festival, Manchester, TN, 12 June 2004)
(6:26)
Hand Me Down HMD43

10-inch vinyl (Numbered limited edition)
The Bucket (2:55)
Slow Night, So Long (3:53)
Wicker Chair (Live at the Roskilde Festival, 3 July 2004) (3:31)
Hand Me Down HMD42

CD
The Bucket (2:55)
Where Nobody Knows (2:23)
Hand Me Down HMD41

iTunes Download
The Bucket (2:55)
Slow Night, So Long (3:53)
Wicker Chair (Live at the Roskilde Festival, Denmark 3 July 2004) (3:31)

Notable variants -
1-track promo CD (Jewel case) - also features track in mp3 format
(BMG 82876 66559 2)
UK 1-track promo (Jewel case) with different artwork
(BMG 82876 64635 2)

Four Kicks
UK release date: 17 January 2005
Highest UK chart position: 24

7-inch vinyl, P/S
Four Kicks (2:09)
Head To Toe (2:04)
Hand Me Down HMD 47

10-inch vinyl
Four Kicks (2:09)
Four Kicks (live In Belgium) (2:46)
Razz (dub Mix) (3:11)
Hand Me Down HMD 46

CD
Four Kicks (2:09)
Head To Toe (2:04)
Hand Me Down HMD 45

Notable variants -
UK 3-track Promo DVD - Four Kicks (Radio)/Four Kicks (Album)/
Four Kicks (Video - Uncensored Director's Cut) (Hand Me Down
HMD44)

King Of The Rodeo
UK release date: 11 April 2005
Highest UK chart position: 41

CD
King Of The Rodeo (2:25)
Taper Jean Girl (Live in Belgium) (3:13)
Molly's Chambers (Live in Belgium) (2:45)
King Of The Rodeo (Video)
Hand Me Down HMD49

7-inch vinyl, P/S (Numbered limited edition)
King Of The Rodeo (2:25)
Soft (live in Belgium) (3:02)
Hand Me Down HMD 50

Notable variants
UK 1-track promo CD, card picture sleeve (Hand Me Down
HMD48)
Australian 1-track promo CD, stickered card sleeve (Sony/BMG
Studios Sydney)

On Call
UK release date: 26 March 2007
Highest UK chart position: 18
(This was the first Kings Of Leon single made available via iTunes
prior to physical release, and was available for download from
6 February 2007)

7-inch vinyl, P/S
On Call (3:28)
My Third House (4:03)
Hand Me Down HMD 51

CD
On Call (3:28)
My Third House (4:03)
Hand Me Down HMD 51

Fans

UK release date: 9 July 2007
Highest UK chart position: 13

7-inch vinyl, P/S

Fans (3:36)
Woo Hoo (3:31)
Hand Me Down HMD 53

CD

Fans (3:36)
Woo Hoo (3:31)
Hand Me Down HMD 53

Charmer

UK release date: 29 October 2007
Highest UK chart position: 85

7-inch vinyl, P/S

Charmer (2:56)
My Party - Chad Hugo/Kenna remix (4:09)
Hand Me Down HMD54

CD (Limited edition)

Charmer (2:56)
My Party - Chad Hugo/Kenna remix (4:09)
Hand Me Down HMD54

Sex On Fire

UK release date: 15 September 2008
Highest UK chart position: 1

7-inch vinyl, P/S

Sex On Fire (3:23)
Beneath The Surface (2:49)
RCA 88697 36890 7

CD

Sex On Fire (3:23)
Knocked Up (live at Oxegen 2008) (7:46)
RCA 88697 35200 2.

Use Somebody

UK release date: 8 December 2008
Highest UK chart position: 2

7-inch vinyl, P/S

Use Somebody (album version) (3:51)
Knocked Up (Lykee Li vs. Rodeo Mix) (5:34)
RCA 88697 41220 7

CD

Use Somebody (album version) (3:51)
Knocked Up (Lykee Li vs. Rodeo Mix) (5:34)
RCA 88697 41218 2

Notable variants

German Limited edition 2-track CD single - sealed and stickered
picture cover with exclusive sweatband. (RCA 88697 49912 2)
German Limited edition 5-track enhanced CD single - features Use
Somebody (album version)/Knocked Up (Lykee Li vs. Rodeo Mix)/
Frontier City/The Bucket (CSS Remix)/Use Somebody (Video)
(RCA 88697 46432 2)

Revelry

UK release date: 2 March 2009
Highest UK chart position: 29

CD

Revelry (album version) (3:21)
Pistol of Fire (Mark Ronson remix) (3:17) (Remix of 2004 track)
RCA 88697 46463 2

Other Releases

Day Old Belgian Blues EP

Release date: 13 June 2006 - distributed with the Belgian music magazine Humo.
Re-issued on 30 June 2009

CD (Limited edition, Digipak)
Taper Jean Girl (3:15)/The Bucket (3:07)/Soft (3:01)/Molly's Chambers (2:45)/Four Kicks (2:41)/Trani (5:44) (all recorded live at the Ancienne Belgique, Brussels, Belgium 4 November 2004

Re-issued as RCA 82876 83362 2

Notion

iTunes download -
Notion (3:00)
Notion (Live in Amsterdam) (3:01)

CD
Exclusive Australian 5-track EP featuring Notion (3:00)/Beneath The Surface (2:49)/Sex On Fire (Live from Cologne) (3:28)/Notion (Live from Amsterdam) (3:01)/The Bucket (CSS Remix) (3:44)

Milk (SNV Edit)

Released: 2006
12-inch white label single-sided bootleg (KINGSOFFULHAM 1)
Stretch'n'Vern remix

K.O.L. EP

Released: April 2009
12-inch vinyl bootleg EP (LEON1)
Sex On Fire (Sharkey Mix)/Use Somebody (Chew Fu Fest Fix) /Use Somebody (Dolby Anol Mix)

INDEX OF SONG TITLES

INDEX